THE WRITER
AS AN ARTIST

For Madelyn —
With warm best wishes
for your work as writer/
artist,

Pat Schreiber

Also by Pat Schneider:

LIBRETTI
The Lament of Michal
Autumn Setting

PLAYS
A Question of Place
Berries Red
Dream: The Musical

POETRY
White River Junction
Long Way Home

NON-FICTION
In Our Own Voices: Writings of Women in
Housing Projects

THE WRITER
AS AN ARTIST

A NEW APPROACH TO WRITING
ALONE AND WITH OTHERS

PAT SCHNEIDER

LOWELL HOUSE
LOS ANGELES
CONTEMPORARY BOOKS
CHICAGO

Schneider, Pat.
    The writer as an artist: a new approach to writing alone
    and with others/ Pat Schneider.
  p.cm.
    Includes index.
    ISBN 1-56565-151-0
    1. Description   I. Title.
  PN145.S265   1993
  808.02—dc20   93-14579
                                          CIP

Lowell House books can be purchased at special discounts when
ordered in bulk for premiums and special sales. Contact
Department V at the address below.

Requests for such permissions should be addressed to:
Lowell House
2029 Century Park East, Suite 3290
Los Angeles, CA 90067

Publisher: Jack Artenstein
General Manager, Lowell House Adult: Bud Sperry
Director of Publishing Services: Mary D. Aarons

Manufactured in the United States of America

10 9 8 7 6 5 4 3 2 1

To
the memory of
Dorothy Dunn,
who said to a seventh-grade girl
in a slum classroom,
You are a writer.

CONTENTS

CHAPTER TEN

Coming Full Circle 232

Acknowledgments

There is a movement in the land to restore to all people the right and privilege of making art with words, including the homey and homely language each of us learned in infancy.

The work I have done alone and in community with hundreds of other writers in Amherst Writers & Artists continues down a path that was begun by pioneer Peter Elbow, who in 1973 dared to publish a book entitled *Writing without Teachers*, in which he challenged the traditional ways of teaching writing that had prevailed then and still do prevail in many places. The work that he has continued to do, and the work of many other writers and artists, goes before and alongside this book.

It is my great privilege to have had Peter Elbow read and respond to the first half of this book when it was in early manuscript. His encouragement and suggestions for change have strengthened the book.

I am grateful for the encouragement and help of my agent, Emilie Jacobson; for the patience and careful insight of my editor, Janice Gallagher, and for the insistence of my friend Sophia Craze that the book be brought to publication.

Many writers in Amherst Writers & Artists have read all or portions of the book, and offered their suggestions for change as well as their own creative work for inclusion. Many of their voices are in these pages; there are many more whom I wish I could have included.

My deepest thanks go to my writing teachers: Dorothy Dunn, Elizabeth Berryhill, Wayne Rood, and Andrew Fetler. And to my writing companion, Margaret Robison. And to hundreds of writers in my workshops in this country, in Ireland, and in Japan, especially Sharleen Kapp in Amherst, Máire O'Donohoe in Ireland, and Nancy Lee in Japan. Last, and most important, my thanks to my greatest teachers: Peter, and our family—Rebecca, Laurel, Paul, and Bethany, my granddaughter Sarah, and my cat, Sister, who kept me company almost every word of the way.

How to Use This Book

This book is designed to be used by a writer working alone or by writers working together. Whether you are a solitary writer, a member of a group, a person who wants to start a writing group, a workshop leader, or a teacher of writing, this book is designed to assist you.

Although Part One, "Writing Alone," is addressed to the solitary writer, it is equally appropriate for writers working in groups. Part Two, "Writing with Others," is addressed to writers in groups but is also intended through story-telling and example to be of interest and help to the solitary writer.

There are 50 writing exercises throughout this book. These are listed, for your reference, in the table of contents. Exercises that pertain to particular aspects of the writing life are offered at the end of appropriate sections or chapters. For example, at the end of Chapter One, "Feeling and Facing Fear," there are two exercises that deal specifically with fear: "Healing the Wounds of Bad Experiences" and "Getting Rid of Internal Critics."

Use this book as it best serves you, whether that means reading straight through or skipping around. Follow the exercises that appeal to you and see if you can adapt others to your particular interests. The pages that follow were written as a kind of love letter from one writer to other writers, and so the book proceeds from one subject to another in the order in which they come up for most of us. It is my hope that each chapter—as in a good collection of short stories or poems—deepens and enriches all of the others, and also stands alone.

A Writer Is Someone Who Writes

I have been a writer all my life. In the fourth grade, at age nine, I wrote my first verse: *"My name is Patsy V./ And I'm in the class 4-B."* In the moments of joy following that creation I was as much a writer as I was at age 45, sitting in Carnegie Hall, hearing the lyric soprano Phyllis Byrn-Julson sing my words: *Gold is gone from the hills,/ The cedar stands grey in the dawn,/ The watchman has gone from the wall./ The heart, the holy place, is empty.* I was not as skilled at nine, but I was as much a writer.

When I was 12, I lived in a tenement in the inner city of St. Louis, Missouri. I would lean out the third-story window at night, dreaming of writing like T. S. Eliot. At 12, I was ironing my mother's starched white cotton uniform every blessed day, but it did not once occur to me that *ironing* could be the subject of literature. This was long before Tillie Olsen had written her story "I Stand Here Ironing." Literature was made by upper-class men, writing their views of the human experience. And I wanted desperately to sound like them so that I could make art, too.

But what I was taught was a lie. Art belongs to the people. It belongs to those who "stand here ironing," to those who clean city streets, to those who work in front of computer screens, as well as to those who read in the ivy halls. Almost all of us can tell a story to a best friend or lover so powerfully that we move the other person to sorrow or to laughter, to deep feeling, to "denouement." You can write as powerfully as you talk. *If you are safe enough.* If you can forget yourself enough, if you can "let go" and tell the truth of what you have experienced or imagined, you can write. If you can tell a tale, if you can make one other person want to listen to you, "see" what you describe, "hear" the voices you repeat, "feel" the end of your story—you can write.

Many of us talk around the supper table, tell stories, jokes, repeat what happened at the office, and never know we are creating fictions, dialogue, suspense, climax. If you can talk, any sense you might have of not being able to write is a *learned disability*. It is almost always the result of scar tissue, of disbelief in yourself accumulated as a result of unhelpful responses to your writing. Those wounds can be healed, those blocks can be removed. Even if you don't talk easily with others but spin out stories in your own head—if you talk to yourself—you can write. You are already an artist; all you have to do is take up your pen and begin.

What I believe is not what everyone believes. It is this: There is no place for hierarchies in the heart, and the making of art is a matter of the heart. Art is the creative expression of the human spirit.

Some artists (some writers) are geniuses. But what is genius made of? I think a large part of it is an amazing self-confidence that enables the genius to reach further, go deeper, take greater risks than a person trapped in fear and self-protection will do. Genius often develops where there is intimate support for it. Shakespeare worked in the intimate, supportive community of a strong theater that wanted his next play. Dickinson worked within the intimate community made up of her family members, who loved her and protected her time and privacy. Where there is no intimate support, there is often the driving force of suffering, creating an intense personal isolation out of which the voice of genius arises. Each of us is capable of genius, but we need support, and we can give it to one another as friends or in honest and supportive workshop settings. Genius is hidden everywhere; it is in every person, waiting to be evoked, enabled, supported, celebrated. It is in you. It is in me. Shakespeare wrote Shakespeare's vision. Dickinson wrote Dickinson's. Who will write yours, if you do not?

Some writers (some artists) are commercially successful. Some artists (some writers) are not. Being commercially successful is a matter of entrepreneurship, luck, and skill. Skill is a wonderful thing; I will work all my life to increase my skill as a writer. But skill is not the same thing as art. Skill is the knowledge of how to mix blue with yellow on my palette, but art is the courage to dip the brush into the paint and lay it on the canvas in my own way. To gain skill is to increase the breadth of what I can do, but art is the depth, the passion, the desire, the courage to be myself and myself alone, to communicate what I and only I can communicate: that which I have experienced and imagined.

For all of us, art is essential, and the making of art can be claimed and experienced. I am convinced that every human being is born an artist and that all literate people are writers who can, if they so desire, claim their writing as a personal (and perhaps public) art form.

I have heard great poems in my workshops. I have heard wonderful short stories, plays, songs, and sections of novels. I am pleased that a good number of them have been published and have received awards, prizes, and national attention. But I am also pleased with many writings that will never be read except by the writer's friends. Those works will never be offered to the public because the writer is too shy, or too uncertain of her or his own abilities, or too awkward at making contacts, or too busy to send off manuscripts, or too bruised by academic grading systems and hostile teacher responses to endure "rejections," or too poor to pay the endless postage, copying fees, and telephone bills that are the startup costs of writing as an entrepreneurial business. The fact that excellent work is unpublished, however, does not diminish its artistry.

I have read literary essays arguing that all truly great works of literature are known to the public. What a cynical and small-minded view of the human spirit! In other times and other cultures, art was made for the family: quilts, hand-carved pieces, lullabies, ballads. The audience for that art was intimate. In a good writing workshop, some exquisite work is given to and received by an intimate audience. I have heard letters and journal entries read aloud in my workshops that I will never forget. Writing is making art, and the test of the value of a work of art cannot be given into the hands of either the commercial world or the academy. Not even the test of time is adequate. A brilliant dance in a small room, unphotographed and unrecorded, is no less a work of art because it was received only by the dozen people present. Art is subjective, personal, miraculous. It happens unpredictably wherever the human spirit is on fire.

I have a writer friend who has led workshops. She once said to me, realizing that I listen to the work of 48 writers each week, several of whom are new or newly returned to writing: "Pat, I don't know how you can stand to listen to all that garbage." It was a helpful comment, because it caused me to stop and evaluate what I do as I listen. My initial response was immediate: "I have never heard a word of garbage in any workshop of mine!" Later, I thought about it and asked myself, Is that true?

It is true. I do listen to frightened people, reading their own written words aloud for the first time since the shame of publicly receiving an "F" on a high school composition. I listen to men who have never before tried to write about feelings. I listen to women coming back to writing for the first time since they left English classes. I hear them trying to sound like Tennyson, Emerson, T. S. Eliot, or some other half-remembered (almost always male) literary model, trying to *write*, not guessing that the rhythms of the language they heard spoken at the kitchen table by their own mothers and fathers are what hold the power of art for them. I hear fear, and hope, and longing. I do not hear any garbage. I hear passion. I hear desire. And when they begin speaking in the mother tongue of their own voices, mining the mother lode of their own stories, the material they and they alone know "by heart," I hear *art*.

I cannot teach anyone to be an artist, but then I don't have to, because everyone is already an artist. Real teachers everywhere know this. Those of us who teach—really teach—know that we are simply midwives to that which is already within our students. Our task is only this: to prepare a place, to welcome, to receive, and to encourage. Most of what we call instruction is simply preparing a place by showing what has been done before—not that it should be copied, but so that options are known, that work which is derivative is recognized, and that all which has preceded us is available as a foundation or as a reference point. Sometimes, if I am careful, I can help an artist recognize her or his own unique voice and come to trust it. But each of us has to claim for our own self this: *I am an artist. I am a writer.*

This is a book about being an artist/writer. Whether your purpose is artistic expression, communication with friends and family, the healing of the inner life, or achieving public recognition for your art, the foundation is the same: the claiming of yourself as an artist/writer and the strengthening of your writing voice through practice, study, and helpful (as opposed to damaging) communication with others.

What you need:
1. To give your art/writing time.
2. To sound more and more like yourself.
3. To experiment, play, take risks, be brave.
4. To believe in the freshness, vitality, and importance of your own experience and imagination.
5. To practice in ways that will teach you to recognize your own voice and to increase its range (as a singer learns to sing higher and lower, as a painter increases the number of colors on a palette).
6. To believe in yourself as an artist-in-training, and to protect yourself from everyone and everything that undermines that belief.
7. To observe.
8. To remember.
9. To imagine.
10. To find and keep in contact with other writer/artists who can provide you with an intimate community of support, give you honest, critical response, strengthen you, and encourage your work.

A writer is someone who writes. The genius in her upstairs room writing "I'm Nobody! Who are you?/Are you—Nobody—Too?" is a writer (Emily Dickinson). The grandmother in a frame house in North Dakota penning a letter on lined paper from Woolworth's is a writer. The child in third grade pushing her pencil to form cursive letters: "T-h-i-s s-u-m-m-e-r i w-e-n-t t-o d-i-s-s-n-y L-a-n-d…" is a writer. You are a writer. You are an artist. Accept it, celebrate it, use it, for the rest of your life.

THE WRITER
AS AN ARTIST

PART ONE

WRITING ALONE

O N E

FEELING AND FACING FEAR

Writing is talking. It is hunkering down around the cave fire at night and telling about the day. And however it may be disguised, close to the center of the first stories we will want to tell is fear. We will tell about the hunt, the animal at the mouth of the cave, the fear that made the mother's arms strong as she protected the child; the wild boar, how it turned and faced the hunter. And as we try to tell our tales, fear will rise. At times, fear keeps us from writing at all, or keeps us from writing as truly, clearly, brilliantly as we might. In this chapter, we will look at the fears that block writing, and take some steps toward overcoming them.

FEAR OF THE TRUTH ABOUT OURSELVES

The first and greatest fear that blocks us as artists is fear of the truth we may discover. The world is familiar to us when it is dressed in our habitual interpretations. It may not be exactly safe, but we know how to walk in it. We can get from sunrise to sunset.

But the unconscious part of us knows more than the conscious mind will admit. When we sleep, dreams hint at our secrets, but in code. Writing, like dreaming, sometimes tells us what we are not ready to hear. What if we suddenly saw our lives, our experiences from a different point of view? What if we glimpsed the face behind the mask, the persona behind the face of mother, of father, of the one we may have forgotten, of the one we may have lost, of the one who made us afraid?

Sarah is beginning to write about her mother. Her father. Her grandmother. She tells me she is having nightmares, and that she is afraid to write because everyone else is so accomplished, so brilliant, and she is such a beginner. I do know that the sense of another's skill can make us timid, but nightmares rise from the depths. They are the guardians of the unconscious. They say, BEWARE, BEWARE, DANGER!

For the writer, fear arises in exact proportion to the treasure that lies shimmering between the dragon's feet. If you are greatly afraid, there is something great to fear. But it is already there, in the unconscious. Writing does not create it. Writing is Adam's task: It gives a name to what was wild. To name the beast is to begin to tame the beast.

In the folklore of magic there is a "spirit familiar." The wild thing that frightens us so when it is hidden, guarded in our unconscious, becomes our spirit familiar when it is named—still full of power, still magical, but power released for us, not power caged and threatening.

I believe the first thing Sarah fears is the truth by which she herself is tempted, the truth of her own vision, her own interpretation of family history, of personal identity. But if she goes straight toward her own truth, what might be lost? Perhaps love is not love, faith is not faith, trust is not worthy. Perhaps a world will be lost. And what will be there to take its place? What price truth?

Everyone has to answer that question for him or herself. I have had both men and women sit in my office and say, "If I go on writing like this I'm going to write myself out of my marriage. I don't know if I can go on." I have seen both men and women writing "fiction" and discovering facts from childhood that altered their understanding of themselves. For some people the choice has been to stop writing, to not pursue expression that will surely take one beyond the known perimeters of the inner world. I respect those who make that choice. Thomas Aquinas, after finishing his massive *Summa*, is purported to have said, "There are some things that simply cannot be uttered." And spent the rest of his life in silence and prayer.

There is an old fairy tale by Hans Christian Andersen about a soldier who goes down into a deep shaft and finds rooms of treasure as he goes deeper and deeper—each treasure greater than the last and each treasure guarded by a dog, each dog having larger and larger eyes. He has a magic apron which allows him to get past the dogs. In the first room he finds copper and fills his pockets; in the second room he finds silver and has to throw away the copper; in the third room he finds gold and has to throw away the silver in order to gather the greater treasure.

It is a metaphor for the process of making art. There is danger in going down into the unknown. What we will find there, in the unconscious where creation happens, may redefine our lives. But I believe we have no other choice if we are to be artist/writers.

For me, the act of writing is a tremendous adventure; it is always a journey into the unknown. It is always fraught with danger. But the deeper we go and the longer we work at our art, the greater our treasure. If you trust your own imagination it will take you past the room where you have gathered copper. The silver you find in the second room will be of far greater worth than copper, and the gold you find in the last and deepest room will make you glad to abandon silver.

Abandonment is a necessary task of the writer. As we grow in our art, our art changes, and we must move on. One of the most generous spirits in contemporary literature is William Stafford, who says the writer's job is to abandon his or her work, to allow others to make judgment of its worth, and to go on to the next poem, the next story. If we cannot let go of old writing habits and old habits of thought, we will not grow as artists. To grow as a writer, we must grow in our capacity to learn, to understand. There is an ancient promise: *You shall know the truth, and the truth shall set you free.* Even those truths that are painful ultimately increase wisdom, undergird strength, make art possible.

The purest and deepest reservoir of material for the writer is his or her own childhood. Most writers, beginning or returning after a long time away from writing, instinctively go to childhood images. This is not accidental, nor is it self-indulgent. It is a good instinct, an artistic wisdom. The writer

Louis Auchincloss believed that "Childhood is the writer's only capital." Flannery O'Connor wrote, "Anybody who has survived his childhood has enough information about life to last him the rest of his days."

Childhood images are remembered for emotional reasons. You may have lost conscious knowledge of the reason why you remember a particular afternoon, but your unconscious mind knows. Childhood images are already polished; the unconscious has already done much of the work of the artist—eliminating what is not important, keeping what is important, transforming it into myth. It is almost as if each memory were a pebble that has been turning in the ocean. If you were to try to write out of what has just happened to you, to try to decide what is important about this day you have just lived, it would be very difficult. There's something about the way our unconscious works, however, that holds for us images that have emotional importance. Even the most random memory is retained as a kind of code for emotional information.

For example, when I was a child I accepted as fact the interpretation of my father given to me by my mother: he was "no good," he never loved me, he abandoned me. I had a few memories of my father, one of which was of myself very small, standing in an outhouse, watching him pee. The memory was still, seemingly random; it was a single picture, like a snapshot, in my mind.

In my mid-40s, my friend, writer/painter Margaret Robison, encouraged me to write about my father and helped me get past my great resistance. After a series of questions, to which I answered that I could not remember anything except the outhouse, Margaret asked me to think about the outhouse. "Tell me what you see," she urged. "What is the wood like? Is it rough or smooth?"

All at once I knew the answer. I saw several things simultaneously. I saw that the wood was rough and unplaned everywhere but where you would sit down, around the holes. There it had been sanded smooth. I saw that there were two holes, one large, one small. I saw that high on one wall, in the corner, there was a nail, and hanging on the nail was a bucket with holes punched in the bottom. This image was clear but made no sense to me.

5

(Days later I asked my mother, "Was there a bucket hanging in the out-house of the place where we lived when my father went away?" And she answered, "Yes, there was, do you remember that?" She explained that they had no running water and took showers by filling the bucket and standing under it as the water ran down through the holes.)

Margaret continued to ask about details of the outhouse. Then she asked, "How do you feel?"

Answering that question was the great breakthrough. All my life I had believed what my mother had told me: that my father did not love me, that he "has another little girl now," that he was "a terrible man." But in the instant following Margaret's question I knew that I had loved him and that he had loved me. I knew that I was safe with him and that I was glad he had taken me out of the house, where suddenly I knew my mother was crying. I was interested by the fact that he urinated standing up, differently from the way I did it, but I was not at all threatened. I felt friendly, cared for, and in good company. At age 45, in a single moment, I knew that when my father left he took with him laughter and lightness. And I gave back to myself the father I had lost at age four.

What astonishes me is how often, if we work carefully and fully, a child-hood image will give up its secret. It does not matter whether we invent as we go. We do, of course. But that doesn't matter, because imagining is another way to get to the truth. And miraculously, if we write clearly and truthfully the images we see in our minds, our readers will also see and will participate by responding with their own emotional experience of the worlds we have presented.

Knowing that the making of art will take us down into dangerous places, what can we do? As artists alone we must be brave. We must have the courage to go into the unknown.

But in the fairy tale, the soldier does not go down into the dark under-ground without some advice and some protection. An old woman shows him the opening in the earth, tells him what he will encounter, and gives him her apron, upon which he is to set each great dog that guards the rooms of treasure. He accepts her help and her magic. As artists in supportive community, we share our wisdom and our experience and help each other complete the solitary journey to find treasure.

There is a last word to be said about the fairy tale. The old woman sends the soldier down into the deep darkness, promising him treasure, but tells him to bring back to her just one thing: an old tinder box. Instead of giving the box to her, he kills the old woman and goes off to have his own adventures with the box and the magical genie inside. This is a complicated ending, but worth a lot of pondering.

Taken as a metaphor for relationships between men and women, youth and age, this fairy tale deals with arrogance, greed, selfishness, and power. It's a pretty grim story. If, however, we take the story as a metaphor for the journey of the writer/artist, perhaps it is telling us that a time comes when we must go on without our parents, our teachers, our mentors, those who first showed us the way. We must go on beyond at least some of our companions. And that necessary individuation—that breaking free—is sometimes very hard, even psychologically violent.

Taken as a metaphor for the inner life, seeing both the soldier and the old woman as parts of one psyche, the story has to do with our tendency, once we have succeeded, to kill off the very part of ourselves that was the source of our art. We despise the dialect we heard at the kitchen table, the folk tales of the family, the peculiar circumstances of our own upbringing.

If every one of us, when we begin to succeed, could continue to honor that in ourselves which is the source of our wisdom and our strength, no matter what it looks like or sounds like, there would not be such fear, such blocks to creativity. And if everyone who succeeded as an artist then turned in humility and grace to help others to succeed, there would be more art, greater art, in the world.

FEAR OF—OR FOR—SOMEONE ELSE

There are very few stories of my own that are not also stories from the life of someone else. And my version of *our story* will always be *my fiction*, my interpretation. What right have I to make fiction of someone else's life?

If I tell the exact truth as I see it, there are two dangers: First, the other will know what I really think—perhaps more than I want him or her to know—and second, what is true for me will probably be untrue for the other. It may not just be a difference of interpretation, either: What I hold as truth may in fact not be true at all.

The fear is fear of loss. I may lose the other's confidence. I may lose the other's respect. I may lose the other's love. I may lose the other.

The fear may also be of lawsuit for libel. Fear of loss of all economic security. Fear of loss of reputation. It may even be fear of loss of life.

To try to write with these fears operating is to try to swim with your hands tied behind your back. It is impossible to get very far, and that only with great struggle and with no power, no grace. Consider, then, the following three steps.

STEP ONE

Accept yourself as a writer and know that you are not alone.

None of us really create *ex nihilo* (out of nothing). All writing involves self-revelation; even if the actual facts of our lives are not revealed, we cannot escape the fact that writing reveals the ways our minds work. All writing is at the least an autobiography of the imagination.

STEP TWO

Understand that all our memories are already fictions.

When I was in graduate school, I wrote a novel for my thesis project in which I included a remarkable character based on my friend and mentor. I described her profession, her great personal power, and used a letter she had written to me as a letter written by the character in the book. Then I sent the manuscript to my friend before I showed it to my academic committee, expecting her to be honored.

8

My friend wrote back that I could use the letter verbatim, but she preferred that I disguise all the facts about her professional identity, etc. I was devastated.

After some time, she guessed my reaction and called me on the telephone. "Pat, you are confusing my wish to be private with a comment on our relationship."

I had to think about that for a long time, but I trusted this friend absolutely, and slowly I came to understand. I changed all the details. I made her into a sculptor and in detail described the sculptor, standing before a lump of clay, sculpting it into the figure of an old woman. As I wrote, I fell in love with the figure my character was sculpting and took my time describing it. It said far more about the character of the sculptor than I myself had known. Never naming her, I created a better, more accurate portrait of my friend.

When the professors on my committee met to discuss the novel with me before my graduation, they agreed that one of the best pieces of writing in the work was the description of the woman sculptor making a figure of an old woman.

Fiction is another way of telling the truth.

STEP THREE

Write it first, fix it later.

Tess Gallagher, in her poem "Each Bird Walking," writes these lines: "Tell me...something I can't forget." And in her introduction to *Best Short Stories of 1983*, Anne Tyler mentions that one of the criteria she used in choosing 20 out of 120 stories was to walk away from them, having read them all, and notice which ones she remembered. Which ones she could not forget.

How do I know what you won't forget? The answer is, you

probably won't forget what I myself can't forget—what is burned most deeply into my own mind.

When I was a young writer I talked to author Elizabeth O'Connor about my work. I told her there were things I could not write about. I would "hurt" my mother. My husband "might not like it." She said, "It sounds to me like there are a lot of absentee landlords of your soul."

Everything that has entered the pupil of your eye, every sound that has entered the inner chamber of your ear, every texture you have touched, every taste, every smell, is yours to rearrange, to re-create. Allow everything your family and friends have given you to be your own; claim it, let it flow onto the page. Then come back to it and decide: Should I disguise? Should I omit? Should I add fictional complications? Should I wait to publish this until my mother is dead? Should I use a pseudonym instead of my own name?

But those aren't the only questions. They aren't even the most important questions. More importantly, ask: Have I gone all the way? Have I traced the shadow along the side of the bright things my eye first saw? Have I told the truth that is the opposite of the habit my mind makes, thinking its usual thoughts?

Don't let your fear of the reaction of others keep you from your first draft. You are the landlord of your own soul. When the words, the memories, the imaginings have finished pouring white-hot onto the page, then you can decide what they are, what they might become, and when their time is to be seen by anyone other than yourself.

Scar-Tissue Fears

More and more now, the creative process is being understood, and truly wonderful things are happening in some elementary school classrooms: Children are being encouraged to learn their spelling and grammar in lessons that are separated from the vulnerable acts of creative writing. Their writing is being taken seriously as self-revelation and is not being subjected to public ridicule and shame by teachers who have no idea that they are destroying the very thing they hope to encourage.

But this has not always been and, unfortunately, still is not always the case. Imagine—or remember—this: You are a child, returning to school on your first day of third-grade. Your teacher, Mrs. Fredericks, tells you to take out a piece of paper and write a paragraph—what you did in the summer just past. You see in your mind your grandma, your grandpa. You write that you went to their house. You helped your grandpa paint the back porch. You went to Disneyland with your grandma. As you hand in your writing, you feel happy and proud. Your teacher gives the paper back to you the next day. Five words are circled with red pencil because they are misspelled. There is an arrow pointing to the place where you forgot to indent the first word of the first paragraph. There are two little lines in red under all the letters that should be capitals. On the bottom is a C-minus.

This is what you learn:

1. You had a C-minus summer. You thought it was an A-plus summer, but it wasn't. It was only C-minus. You have a C-minus grandma and grandpa, or worse, they are A-plus, but you have failed to show that they are A-plus. You have failed your grandma and your grandpa.

2. Mrs. Fredericks didn't want to know about your summer after all. What she wanted to know was whether you could spell *grandma* and *Disney,* whether you remembered about indentation and capitalization.

3. Never, never again write about something that matters deeply to you. Protect what is personally important. Just find out what the teacher wants, and then write that.

Mrs. Fredericks is a nice person. She does not mean you any harm. She herself was injured when she tried to write. She herself has suffered the silencing of judgment. She does not know that she is passing on the damage that was done to her long before this day. But the next time she asks you to write about a vacation, you will not see your grandma's face. You will see little letters lined up—*V,* you will write, and then erase it, place it indented,

11

and make it a better capital; *a*, you will write, then *c,a,t,i,o,n*. You will have learned to spell *vacation*, and you will have learned that telling your own vision, the truth of what your inner eye sees, is something you must not ever do again.

At the end of this chapter you will find two writing exercises that I have used in workshops, and that you can use to get in touch with some of the history that is hidden under your writing blocks. They are titled: "Healing the Wounds of Bad Experiences" and "Getting Rid of Internal Critics."

FEAR OF SUCCESS

After a session of my writing workshop at the Graduate Theological Union in Berkeley, during a discussion over dinner about the fears that block us, Sister Consuelo Pacheco spoke about the fear of success. Consuelo had written about growing up as a Mexican-American, accused by schoolchildren of being different, and ridiculed even by teachers for her accent. I was surprised by her comment about fear of success, and I asked her to write out her thoughts for my book. She titled this piece "If I Succeed."

If I succeed, my work will be public; I will be public. My work will be viewed by sophisticated, educated people who know what they're talking about, who will expect answers I don't have, and who will pry deeper, as if what I have revealed is not enough. They will demand more, and I'm afraid I won't be able to deliver. They will find out what a big fake I am; I, myself, will find out that I am not THAT deep, THAT profound. I will have to be super aware of my presentation before others. I will be forced to promote myself, to parade my achievements. I will have to deal with professional critics. My craftsmanship will be dissected and what is important to me will be dismissed or trivialized. I am not afraid of losing my work; I am afraid of losing my soul. I will have to give up old familiar not okay feelings and thoughts. I don't

know if I can live with happiness and bliss. I am afraid of the new.
If I succeed, I will be successful and I am afraid of what that will
mean.

Fear of success is frequently a problem for women who have been raised to be "good" girls, obedient, knowing and keeping to their place. It is also a problem for persons struggling to get out of poverty, out of racially or culturally defined limitations, such as those experienced by Consuelo.

I have led a workshop for eight years for women in low-income housing projects. Elizabeth, a beautiful young woman who with the group's encouragement had returned to school and completed her college work, was offered a high-paying job at a local hospital. She called me, very excited and happy about the opportunity. But two days later, another woman in the workshop called to tell me, "Pat, Elizabeth has taken her entire paycheck from her part-time job and bought cocaine. She took it—all of it. What can we do?"

I knew Elizabeth well; I had watched her grow and change. I was absolutely certain that what had happened to her was a panic attack caused by the fear of success. After all, if she were to really succeed, she would be a different person. She would live in another kind of house, have different friends, even dress differently. I remembered a time in college when a professor had given me money to meet a crisis in my family that threatened my staying in school. I told the other woman to go to Elizabeth and tell her that I was putting a check in the mail for the full amount of her week's pay. "Tell her," I said, "that it never happened. Tell her to get up in the morning and begin again. It never happened."

To this day, Elizabeth and I have never directly mentioned that money, nor that temporary breakdown. She took the job, and she has kept it. She has moved out of the projects, and is a successful professional woman. In facing the fear of success, as in facing all the other fears, we need the support of friends who understand.

13

THE FEAR OF FEAR ITSELF

After a long time of trying and of meeting walls of inner silence, there can come about a self-perpetuating pattern. Fear breeds fear, increases, and can become the source as well as the product of itself.

There is a simple solution. There is an "open sesame." It is so clear and so simple, it may seem like a gimmick. If so, fine—who cares? It works.

Never, never, never say to yourself, "I am going to write a poem." Never say, "I am going to write a story." Or a play. Or a novel, for God's sake. Just lift your pen and write down a single, specific, concrete image you see in your mind. Describe it in extreme detail. The more specific and intimate, the better. A crack in a coffee mug. A vein on the back of your hand. The way a lock of hair falls across the forehead of a child as she sits reading. A single hair that grows at an awkward angle from the eyebrow of an old man who is fishing. Get in close, describe a detail, and don't allow yourself to predict where it is going to go. Go from one detail to another. Skip around. Abandon one thing when another appears in your mind.

Richard Hugo, in his book *The Triggering Town*, writes about how one image triggers another. Most of his poems begin with a town. For him, it must be a town of a particular size—not too big, not too small. Then he jumps to something else, and when the poem is done he often goes back and removes the town.

What Hugo is talking about, I believe, is central to the process of creative writing. When we are writing, the disconnections are as important as the connections. One image triggers another, and like a person walking on large rocks across a creek where the water is fast and slippery, we will not get to the fifth rock that allows us to step onto the opposite bank unless we first step on, and then abandon, rocks number one, two, three, and four. Remember the fairy tale of the soldier: Copper led him to silver, and silver led him to gold. So it is with writing. The first image that comes may not be the treasure I am after. I may begin with describing a hairline crack in a coffee mug, and in saying the crack is black with age, I may suddenly be reminded of an ancient crack in a glacier I once looked into in Alaska. I see the blue there, deeper and colder than any blue I have ever seen since. If I do not abandon the mug and go faithfully to the blue ice, I will not get to the blue stone someone gave me when I was young. If I do not abandon the blue ice when the blue stone appears, I will not get to the story of the evening when a young man gave me the blue stone, said he could not marry me, and told me why. Only when I get to that story will nothing else interrupt me. I will be there, in that evening, and nothing else will matter as I write what he said, what I said, and how the stone was as blue and as cold as ice. I will not need to ask whether the form should be story or poem or novel or play. Ben Shawn, the visual artist, has written a book called *The Shape of Content* in which he says, "Form is the shape of content." It is as true of writing as it is of painting: If I am true to the content, the form will take care of itself.

Our best, our deepest ideas often do not come to us first. We have to follow a kind of trail, allow images to come and go, sketch as visual artists sketch, until we get to the picture that holds us, that will not let us go.

William Wordsworth's words sound a little archaic now, but what they say is true: "Poetry is emotion recollected in tranquillity." Making art with our words is emotion remembered in the solitary act of writing. As we write, we re-create images, and the emotion is re-created within the images, both for ourselves and for those who dream after us the images we have recorded on the page.

Once you have begun to trust this way of writing—this magical "open sesame" of beginning with the intimate detail and trusting the disconnections—it will become perfectly clear how impossible, how absurd it is to ask a roomful of people, "All right, class, now write a story." Or to say to a friend, "There's a sunset. Write a poem." If the sunset is right there, why should the friend *write* a sunset? Writing doesn't come like that. It comes up from memory, and it skips like a flat stone across the water until finally it sinks into the depths where wonderful monsters and beautiful creatures dwell.

Healing the Wounds of Bad Experiences

All of us have been wounded in our self-esteem as writers. No matter how successful we may have been, or how we may protest that we can "take it," the act of writing is self-exposing and makes us vulnerable. All of us carry around some scar tissue that operates as a block to freedom in our writing.

This exercise is designed to put you back into places where you had experiences that formed you as a writer. If you can write those experiences, let them happen again on your page, you may find that you can now understand them, heal the wounds, and dissolve your blocks.

Sit in a comfortable place where you will have privacy and silence. Prepare your paper, have your pen ready, lay them aside within easy reach. Do all you can to make yourself comfortable. For me, this would mean a steaming cup of something hot, a chair big enough to curl my leg under me, and a window nearby with sun. Make yourself as comfortable, as safe, as you can. After all, you are going in search of things which have hurt you; you deserve all the help you can give yourself.

Now, read the rest of the exercise and then close your eyes and do it in your own way.

With your eyes closed, take a few minutes to let various parts of your body relax. I find this is easiest when I consciously give some gratitude to my body. I have friends who have suffered—even died—from terrible maladies; I am grateful to my body for its strength. I can say to my feet, thank you for carrying me around. Be at ease now.

If you find this silly, then don't do it. Find your own way to relax, but I begin with my feet. They are farthest away from my head, where I spend so much of my energy. They seem to need my attention first and most when I want to gather myself in, become unified, centered. Once, a writer in my workshop, a professor of sports history, told me I should begin with the rhythms of breathing, rather than with my feet. We ultimately agreed—I should begin with my feet; she should begin with her breath.

When you have centered, relaxed, just let your mind travel back across your life to another time, before this time, and find yourself in front of school. Open the door; go in. What do you smell? What is the quality of light when the door closes behind you? Now walk to your classroom, open the door, go in. What does your eye see? Who is there? Is anything written on the blackboard? What does the room smell like? What is the quality of light in the room?

Take your seat. The teacher is going to tell you to take out a piece of paper and do some creative writing. Allow that to happen. Be aware of how you feel.

Stay there as long as you want. If anything begins to happen, let it happen. Notice any detail your inner eye sees; every detail is important. When you are ready, open your eyes and pick up your pen and paper. Write what your inner eye sees, or what happened, or anything else that comes to you to write.

Note: There is nothing sacred about this or any exercise. If this exercise does not work for you, adapt it to a form that feels more comfortable to you. Perhaps you would actually be more relaxed if you went to a corner booth in your favorite coffee shop, kept your eyes open, let the jukebox drive out the conversations of others, and imagined yourself back in a classroom. If your significant experiences with early writing were somewhere other than the classroom, go there in your imagination and write what happened.

One woman in my workshop named Diana Coccoluto insisted she could not write because she did not see images. She claimed she had ideas, but no images.

I found this hard to believe, and asked her to try this exercise. She talked with me later about what happened. She saw herself walking into the school, heard the teacher's instructions, took out her paper and pen. She heard the teacher tell her to write about home. In her fantasy she was a young child. She sat for a little while, and other children around her began to write. She had an overwhelming fear of writing about home. Deliberately she overturned her inkwell, letting the ink spill across her paper.

Then she opened her eyes but did not write. "See?" she said to me. "I didn't have any images."

But what an image—this little girl turning over her inkwell and the ink running down the desk and across the paper and onto her dress! Yet Diana did not recognize it as an image because she was too afraid to own the ones she did have. What she described to me were powerful images. I told her several times that if she had written what she had spoken, it would have been strong, moving writing.

Gradually she began to write in the workshop. At first she did not read to the whole workshop; that was too frightening. At first she gave her work to me alone and later to the workshop. What she wrote was the story of a terrified child who was being sexually abused, terribly mistreated, forced to do the work of an adult, forced to care for younger siblings in a cruel home environment. The image she had first seen of a child too frightened to write about home, pouring ink out on the page to avoid writing the words that would tell the truth of her suffering, was a brilliant image, a powerful metaphor for the silencing of the truth.

In another workshop, Diane Smithline wrote the following in response to this exercise:

I'm just a kid. It's recess in eighth grade. The time when Mr. Finan hands back papers. He leaves them on the top of our desks. I am fooling around with my friends, but really I am waiting for him to come to my desk. I have opened my heart to him in a poem about my father's sudden death.

Nonchalantly I walk over to my newly varnished desk with the top that lifts up and the inkwell we never use. With nervous anticipation I read the only words he has written on my paper: *The margins are too narrow.*

The room recedes. A silence drops over me. I am totally alone. I sink into my chair stunned, a quivering wounded animal. My back curves downward. My head bends. I see my fingers trace the circle of the inkwell around and around.

I am smaller.

Diane's closing words are a brilliant summary of what happens to us when work we have written out of utmost vulnerability is given a careless or harsh response. I encouraged her to try breaking these lines into poem form, and the workshop affirmed the power of the writing. Gradually Diane's own voice came back to her, larger and stronger as she healed the wound of that bad experience.

All of us who have, in Flannery O'Connor's words, "survived…childhood," have painful memories. Life gives us those. Even in the best of homes and schools, things happen that hurt us. Some of the hurts may fester under the surface and cause a blocking of our artistic expression. Blocks are real; they are the tips of icebergs. But in the right kind of warm attention, they can be melted.

EXERCISE 2:
Getting Rid of Internal Critics

This exercise, suggested to me by Jim Eagan, a writer in my workshop, is wonderful for becoming aware of the community of critics (and, if we're lucky, supporters) we all carry around in our heads. What a cacophony of invisible nay-sayers many of us accommodate all the time! Without knowing it, when some writers take pen to paper at, say, age 52, their own Professor Pompous, alive and well in the mind after 30 years of physical absence, instantly retorts, "Who do you think you are? You haven't ever finished that incomplete I gave you in Dumbbell English 101!" And the pen falters, the interior vision dries up, the block sits solidly in place. This exercise can give Professor Pompous at last his opportunity to scream out onto the page his whole miserable speech and can give you the opportunity to tell him you don't give a bleep about his incomplete and tell him where to go.

If this seems silly to you, try it anyway. Your invisible critic is probably not Prof. Pomp. at all—she may very much surprise you when she appears.

As in Exercise 1, prepare a place for yourself. You will need a good, long writing time for this exercise, so try it at night or unplug the telephone and pretend you're not at home. Give yourself time. In the way that is most comfortable for you, center your attention and relax.

When you have finished your centering, imagine yourself on a wide stretch of prairie or desert. You can see all the way to the horizon. You are standing beside a road. The little road meanders along, winding, curving, stretching from the horizon all the way to in front of your very feet and past you into the distance.

Far, far in the distance, you can see a bus coming toward you. Let it come slowly. Perhaps there are heat waves that make it shimmer a bit at first. Let it come closer, and closer, until it draws up alongside you and stops.

The door opens, and people come out one by one. Each person who gets off the bus is someone who has an opinion about your writing. (Mother? Father? Sister? Brother? Sixth-grade teacher? Professor of English? Editor who recently rejected your manuscript? Best friend who has a huge ego and got published last month?) The "loudmouths" push off the bus first. Let them off, one by one, and let each one say what is on her or his mind. Write it down. If you want, note how the person is dressed; write that down. After all the loudmouths get off, there will be some quiet folk at the back of the bus. Let them off, too. What they have to say may be entirely different.

After you have written the speeches of the people on the bus, you may want to do a dialogue with one or more of them.

Consuelo Pacheco, who wrote the piece above on fear of success, is a visual artist as well as a writer. Here is a small portion of her response to this exercise:

Watchers and Other Creeps

The familiar rickety old yellow bus is a tiny dot on the horizon. As it approaches I know that this time I am ready for them. I

20

don't have a long pen that I could use as a spear and I don't have my carving and modeling tools, good eye pokers though they might be. This time all I do have is ME: one hundred thirty pounds, five feet three quarters inch of pure *lumbre Chicana:* FIRE!

The bus shrieks. The riders are agitated and noisy. They begin to get off the bus. I am ready! My feet are planted solidly on the ground.

"CONE-SWAY-LOW," Miss Phigpus pushes the syllables through her puckered-up flabby lips as she looks at me. "How sweet you look. But don't take any pencils or paper home because you'll lose the pencil and get the paper all messed up. Mexican children are dirty, not like the children in Dopra, Wisconsin."

"*Consuelo, vida mia,*" Nona smiles. "You have more talent in one little finger than most girls have in their whole bodies, and you, YOU make me so mad when you don't use it! Don't just stand there! Do something! Move! But, don't move too fast and don't do anything too well or make anything too beautiful. I don't want you to become famous. That's too much power for a woman. *Una mujer poderosa es una mujer peligrosa.* Why, a powerful woman can burn a whole town."

Consuelo wrote on, page after page of voices. And then, suddenly, she began to answer them: "Nona, Nona, you were so important to me. Your words were Gospel Truth. How dare you give me mixed messages about what YOU were afraid of: POWER, LOVE, SEX, CHILD BEARING, LIFE..." Finally, after answering all the other voices, she wrote, "And now, Miss Phigpus. How I wanted to love you, Miss Phigpus, and how I hated you for years and years. Get the hell out of my head; get the hell out of my heart and off my back! When I was little you poured your racism and your white supremacy crap on me. Well, take your crap back!"

This exercise is a powerful tool for discovering and laying to rest those internal voices that still block us when we try to write. The bumper sticker that proclaims "IT'S NEVER TOO LATE TO HAVE A HAPPY CHILDHOOD" could be adapted for us writers: IT'S NEVER TOO LATE TO GET RID OF THE INTERNAL CRITICS.

TWO

GETTING STARTED (AGAIN)

Almost everyone has at some time been a writer. A writer is someone who writes. You have done it; you have expressed yourself on paper. Getting started is almost always picking up an old dream, an old desire. Getting started is usually getting started *again*. And only you can discover what you need to get going.

There is a category of question I have heard some writing teachers ridicule: What kind of pen do you use when you write? Do you write your first drafts on lined paper or blank? Do you write at a typewriter or computer or with a pencil or fountain pen? Do you write in the daytime or at night?

Questions about the intimate details and habits of the writing life are not irrelevant; they come from an instinctive knowledge that these are important matters. The answers have to do with getting started, with keeping going. Each of us has idiosyncrasies, habits, inclinations, and those peculiar traits are often linked closely to our creativity. Therefore these questions—and their answers—are important.

So, what do *you* need? You need to discover and respect your own rituals and habits so that they will assist you rather than block and frustrate you. You need space, privacy, and time, and you need to be constantly learning, growing. You need to know how to begin again.

RESPECT YOUR OWN PATTERNS

Each of us has certain patterns connected to our creative work. They are the habits, the rituals, we have developed as ways to access our own artistry. According to legend, the composer Niccolò Paganini could compose only if he had a blanket over his head. Well? Who cares? What wonderful music he composed under his blanket! Some of what the writer in you needs will be dictated by your psychological history and makeup. If you, too, need the ritual of placing a blanket over your head to do your art, then claim your blanket! The way you go about it is your own business; what matters is that you get the writing onto the page.

Once I was on the staff of a conference with an older, much loved writer. She carried a small, beautifully bound note pad with her everywhere and frequently wrote notes to herself in it. The words she wrote were visible from a distance; she printed in very large, block letters. I overheard someone asking her why she wrote so large—did the large print help her in some way, later, when she used the notes in her writing? She smiled and answered no, it had nothing to do with her writing. She printed in large letters because her eyesight was poor, and it was easier to read that way. Some of your patterns for doing your writing most effectively will be dictated by the needs of your physical body.

Many of your patterns will be dictated by your aesthetic taste. I write most comfortably by a window. I have friends who are distracted by the motions of birds and tree branches and prefer to write facing a blank wall. I like to have what I call my own "sacred objects" (stones, feathers, pictures, keepsakes) around me. They seem full of spirit, numinous familiars in the writing space. My husband, Peter, needs a cleared desk: no pictures, nothing but his work before him.

Some of your patterns will be dictated by your surroundings. My writer friend Sharleen Kapp writes with the television on. She lives alone; the television keeps her company. It would drive me crazy. Another friend goes to a local greasy-spoon hamburger joint, orders a cup of coffee, and writes for hours. She finds more privacy there than at home with husband, sons, dog, telephone, dishwasher, et cetera.

Anne Brudevold, a writer in my Amherst workshop, has this to say:

> My writing goes best and I'm happiest when I write with what I think of as my "soft mind." My soft mind doesn't focus on maintaining any particular line of thought, but is quite receptive, and I think this is why my surroundings are important to me when I write. Sometimes I like to write in places that hold some kind of relationship to what I'm writing about. Then the things that happen around me incorporate themselves into what I'm writing and help move it along. I pick up on the energy of the place and/or people, and get ideas that wouldn't otherwise come to me.
>
> I've written in barbershops, restaurants, train stations, just to name a few, but my favorite place to write is the farm where I keep my horse. There for me real time stops. I can walk out into the pasture, or down the aisle of the barn and ideas start spinning that I want to write down. Stories unfold themselves in details of hay, machinery, animals, and the people who live, work, and visit there. The stories may have nothing to do with the reality of the place. They may be spinoffs, germinated there, but completely transformed in some mysterious way I don't understand. It seems effortless, almost like a game, but with a very sweet sense of connectedness to real people and events and their very long and complex histories. Sometimes I imagine that these people are not only in my stories, but that I'm writing for them. They are my audience, and that helps me set the tone and choose the words.

We are each unique, and not all circumstances help us to write. What is important is not how someone else writes, but that you should become acquainted with your own patterns, respect them, and provide for yourself so that they will assist you.

GIVE YOURSELF SPACE AND PRIVACY

For many women, the struggle to write is basically a struggle against a cultural assumption that women's lives are of no interest as literature. I have a woman friend whose husband, after her first book had been published, commented, "You sit there writing as if your life had some significance."

For many men, the struggle to write is basically a struggle against a cultural assumption that it is not "manly" to reveal the inner life, the secrets of the heart and of the imagination.

For both men and women in our society, the act of self-revelation is an act of great courage. Self-revelation is essential to the writer: man, woman, or child. And self-revelation requires solitude. Franz Kafka wrote to Felice Bauer:

> For writing means revealing oneself to excess; that utmost of self-revelation and surrender, in which a human being, when involved with others, would feel he was losing himself, and from which, therefore, he will always shrink as long as he is in his right mind—for everyone wants to live as long as he is alive—even that degree of self-revelation and surrender is not enough for writing. Writing that springs from the surface of existence—when there is no other way and the deeper wells have dried up—is nothing, and collapses the moment a truer emotion makes that surface shake. This is why one can never be alone enough when one writes, why there can never be enough silence around when one writes, why night is not night enough. This is why there is never enough time at one's disposal, for the roads are long and it is easy to go astray...

Once, when I was a young playwright, I received a full scholarship for three weeks in a hotel room in the theater district in New York City. I was given complete freedom, solitude in the private room all day, and free theater tickets to major shows in the evenings. I loved the shows. It should have

26

been heaven. I did learn, and it was valuable. But the days were a nightmare. I have never in my life been more blocked than I was in that square, ugly room with a window looking out onto a brick wall.

Virginia Woolf has said it: What a woman, what any writer, needs to write is a room of one's own. It is not simply a matter of space—it is a space of one's own that is needed. My problem as a young writer in New York City was that I didn't know how to make the space my own.

Now, when I go away to write (and I do, several times a year) I take with me a few objects that help me to connect to my own inner voice: the marble that I found washed up on the beach near Rockport, Massachusetts, years ago. The petrified snail shell given to me by my writer friend. A candle and matches. My favorite pen and my old, familiar journal notebook. And I know how to get started now; what to do first, what to do second. Not because it is the right way for anyone else, but because I have caught myself in the act of getting going, I have watched my patterns, and I know what works for me.

Robin Therrian, one of the writers in my Chicopee Workshop for women in low-income housing projects, has given each of her children a blank book and told each child it is his or her own; they do not touch her journal and she does not touch theirs. Robin is saying to her children, each of whom cannot have a room alone, "Be free, be respectful, be yourself." She is teaching them to value their own opinions, their own right to honest expression. In giving them journals and the certainty that she will not read them, she is giving them encouragement to write and the privacy they must have if they are to become artists. A writer must have *a room of one's own*. Where it is impossible to have a physical room with a door to close, one must nevertheless have privacy; space, that is, where the writer can be free, can be himself or herself, can exorcise the ghosts of bad teachers and fearful parents and competitive friends and rejecting editors—all those absentee landlords of the soul.

The problem of space and privacy takes different forms for the person who is working outside the home and the person who is the primary caregiver to small children and/or aging or disabled family members. In either case, how can that person write down the mind's dream, find the energy and the emotional centeredness necessary for artistic creation? How is one to combat the demons of depression and the frustration of repeated failure to find time, space, solitude, focus, concentration?

My own pattern of claiming for myself a necessary solitude was conditioned by my generation's habits and assumptions. When I left home in 1952, it was to go to a double room in a dormitory at college and graduate school, and from there to marriage and children. From age 10, I kept a diary—later, a journal in a loose-leaf notebook—and wrote wherever there was an empty chair or a corner of a table. The time came, however, when I was overwhelmed by mothering. With three preschool-aged children, two still in diapers, I finally said to myself, "It is over. I will never write again." I packed my typewriter away in the back of a closet in an upstairs bedroom. I quit.

On a particular winter afternoon I felt as if I would lose my mind. It was a day when all three babies were fussy, and nothing I could do was enough. We were all in the kitchen, which was cluttered with toys, baby formula, laundry, and breakfast dishes. Condensation on the windows closed all access to the outside world. A very painful kind of cry began in my mind. It was rhythmic, like a chant. In that desperation where one does not observe oneself, I ran out of the kitchen, up the stairs two at a time, grabbed the typewriter, brought it down, and slammed it on top of the throbbing washing machine—the only cleared surface in the kitchen. With two babies playing on the floor and one strapped to the changing table, I pounded out a page-long poem. Although it did not say so directly, the meaning was "I will never write again." When I finished, I stood in a kind of shock, knowing three things: I had been writing; what I had written was not bad; and nothing, as long as I lived, would keep me from writing again.

For years I kept a typewriter in the kitchen. It sat on the ironing board, on the kitchen counter, on the dish cabinet. It sat on a kitchen chair. But it was there, all the time, and there was always paper in it, and often there were words coming and going on the pages.

Only after my children (ultimately four) were all in public school did I set up a desk of my own in a corner of the bedroom I shared with my husband.

There were drawers in the desk—space to myself! I was growing in my sense of my own needs, but so slowly. Several years later I moved into half of a basement room where my husband and I set up a partition between our two desks. I had gone from a desk of my own to half a room of my own. It wasn't enough; I had no protection from his telephone conversations, the sounds of his work—but it was an improvement.

Everyone differs, but what kept me from having a room of my own is common. It was not so much the difficulty of finding space as it was my own attitude: I saw others' needs as more important than my own.

It was after my 50th birthday that I decided to take money from my teaching income, go into town, and rent an office space of my own. The office I chose was sunny, clean, and utterly private. For several weeks I refused to move any furniture in; I just went there, locked the door behind me, and sat on the floor in a square of sunlight, soaking up solitude. Having my own space away from home was one of the most blissful experiences of my entire life. Gradually I claimed it as work space, moved into it the things I needed to be able to do my work. I kept the office space for three years and learned what I needed to know about myself in order to be able to claim a space of my own at home that would be truly mine—not a space in which I felt I was staking out illegal squatter's rights, but a space that was deeply, spiritually, a room of one's own. When I gave up the office space, I took out a building loan, remodeled a room at home into a studio, put in great, wonderful windows and a heavy-duty soundproof door, and here I sit typing these words in a room—inner and outer—of my own.

If you have not yet claimed and made for yourself a room of your own, begin to do so. Do what is possible, love it, and use it, and dream of the day when you can take the next step. The first "room" of my own was a few lines each day in a five-year diary. From that little seed grew the studio in which I work today.

Writing takes time as well as space. Like other art forms, the act of writing can and must take your whole attention; time collapses, disappears, seems to dissolve. It is actually a wonderful experience, but it can happen only if you create a safe environment for concentration. No telephone interruptions. No friendly chats with members of the family about matters of little consequence. There is further discussion of this subject in Chapter Three, "Toward a Disciplined Writing Life."

GROWING AS A WRITER

No one can teach another person how to write. Joseph Campbell said, "Where there is a path, it is someone else's way." No one can, in the deepest sense, teach another how to create.

And yet we must learn. We must continue to learn, to grow as writer/artists as long as we live. And we can help one another to learn.

Learn by Finding a Good Teacher

When I was young I spent one year at a small college in Nashville, Tennessee. While I was there, I heard about a famous group of poets across the street at Vanderbilt University. They were called the Hermitage School of Poets, and I wanted to study with them. At my own school, a teacher advised me to stay away from them. "They are called a 'school' of poets because they all sound alike," he said. "Don't go. They won't value your work unless you change it to fit their ideas of what a poem should be." I followed his advice, not only that year, but for the rest of my life. I have tried to study with teachers who do not use their own style of writing as a standard by which to measure the work of others.

A good teacher helps you to sound more and more like your own self, less and less like him or herself, less and less like the so-called great writers of the past. The test is simple: When you come away from a session with your teacher, do you feel more or less like writing? Do you find yourself invigorated, challenged, energized for the task of revision and development of your work, or do you find yourself embarrassed, humiliated, and discouraged? The issue is not whether the teacher is tough or gentle, cruel or kind; the issue is the effect on you, on your work. A teacher who is good for you may be a terrible teacher for your best friend. Finding a good teacher is certainly as sensitive and miraculous as finding a good doctor or a good therapist or a good minister. A good teacher causes your work to grow, deepen, freshen, increase. If the opposite is happening, know that you are taking into yourself a kind of poison that in time will kill your art. Escape as quickly as you can.

A good teacher gives you an honest (and sometimes hard to hear) response but acknowledges that all responses are subjective. He or she encourages you to listen to other opinions and take only that "criticism" which strengthens and encourages your own voice, your own deepest intention, your own unique vision. A good teacher shares with you something of her or himself, does not stand on a pedestal, engages you with affection.

A good teacher for you is a teacher who likes your work. If he or she cannot identify the strength in your writing voice, then she or he cannot address what is mitigating that strength. This is a very important point. Do not subject yourself to any teacher who gives you only negative feedback. That person is suffering from a needy ego and will feed on your destruction. A good teacher knows more than you do, is willing to pass on to you what he or she knows, and will rejoice when you find your own way of using what you have been given.

Writing and teaching are not the same skill and do not always inhabit the same human body. Good writers are not necessarily good teachers. Many students travel great distances and often move across the country to study with their favorite writer, only to discover that what that writer does on the page is not at all reflected in what he or she does in the classroom. There are great writers who cannot teach and great teachers of writing who do not themselves write or are not acclaimed writers. There are teachers who are geniuses, and there are teachers who are fools.

All of us must suffer some fools. If you are in school, you do not always have the luxury of choosing your teachers. Learn from everyone; even those you do not like can teach you how *not* to teach. Above all, trust your own voice, your own intuition, your own artist self. The person who taught me most about writing poetry in graduate school was not the famous poet on the faculty but my fellow student, Margaret Robison. She cared deeply about my work, evoked it, challenged it, and encouraged me to grow. Claim as your teacher the person who best helps you to write, and to write better. Ask yourself this: After a session with my teacher, do I feel more or less like writing?

Learn by Reading Other Writers

Next to fear, the most common handicap I have seen in writers who are beginning again is that often we do not know the writing of our own contemporaries. As a result, we take for our (largely unconscious) models the work of writers long dead, writers whose sensibility and use of the language has become outdated. Just as it pains me to remember how I, as a 12-year-old in the slums of St. Louis, Missouri, wanted to sound like a middle-aged male poet in England, so it pains me to see a young New England writer unconsciously imitating the language of long-dead poets whom he studied in high school and in college. Work modeled on these so-called classic poets often uses general language, abstract words, and archaic contractions that were in style when the poet was writing but sound vague or even silly now. This is not the writer's fault; he or she has no idea that "literature" can be absolutely contemporary, that stories can be written in the voice of the street language we hear on the subway and poems in the voice of the mother at home as she braids the hair of the child who sits on the kitchen stool.

We are beginning to understand that the models of the accepted canon can be problematic, especially for women and people of color. As late as the mid-1970s, when I spent four years working on an MFA in creative writing at the University of Massachusetts, there was not a single female or non-white faculty member in the program. The writers we were required to read were still largely white and male. At that time the canon included an incredibly small proportion of writers who were women or people of color. By my own request, I took a course in Virginia Woolf taught by Lee Edwards, a woman professor outside the MFA program. Reading Woolf changed my life. When I read *To the Lighthouse* and *The Waves* I felt as if I was hearing my own mother tongue for the first time, and I had not even known I was living in exile. I had read James Joyce, T. S. Eliot, Carl Sandburg, Walt Whitman, William Faulkner, and on and on. But even as

32

late as 1979, at age 45, having completed master's degrees in religious studies and theater and an MFA in creative writing, and living an easy walk from
Emily Dickinson's home, I was nevertheless profoundly ignorant of the
work of women writers. It is not that we cannot learn from the dead; it is
that the accepted canon has been too narrow, the voices of women and
nonwhites too marginalized, the received standards of excellence too self-
perpetuating.

I do not know the answer to the question now being wrestled to the
ground by feminist scholars and debated by women writers. Is there such a
thing as a distinctly woman's voice? One writer says yes, another says no. All
I know is that for me, reading all of the fiction and most of the nonfiction of
Virginia Woolf oriented me to the possibility of my own voice in a way that
had never occurred in a lifetime of reading the work of famous men. It was
the beginning of my own personal writing revolution.

It is absolutely necessary to read the work of your own generation, your
own gender, your own color, your own class—voices that are close to your
own life choices and experience—as well as voices of writers of the past and
writers of difference. Try expanding your reading habits, too. Read aloud,
walking; read onto tape and listen as you drive; memorize work that you
love. Those writers whose work you love will be your best teachers. If you
love a certain writer's work, the chances are he or she would be interested
in yours; no doubt there are some things you have in common, some things
you could share. Develop your tastes. You don't have to like every writer
whose work appears in *The Best Short Stories of 19—*. Read as you might
listen, turning a radio dial. Try different "stations" and go on until you find
something you really like. When you find a story or a poem you like, read it
more than once. Read it as a writer, watching how it works, what the author
is doing. The writers you love will teach you how to write, if you read them
thoughtfully, watching, catching them "in the act." They will give you permission to try new things; they will open doors in your own mind, if you will
let them.

HOW TO GET STARTED (AGAIN)

The moment comes to put pen on paper and begin to form words. How does it happen? Especially if you haven't been writing for some time, or if you are feeling dry or blocked—how do you begin?

Begin Gently—Write in Your Journal

Whenever I have been away from my writing for a long time, the path back feels tangled and daunting, as if I am at the edge of a jungle without my machete. Most often, I begin by writing just for myself. This kind of writing was once considered an important art form. People kept journals or diaries. Many still do, even though they may not talk about it. My druggist keeps a daily journal of bird calls. A priest I know keeps two journals: one is on his desk, one is hidden and locked. Journal keeping and its importance for the writer will be discussed more fully in Chapter Four. Often, the way I start to write is something very simple, a kind of diary entry: "December 1. Yesterday I went to Northampton, looking for a birthday gift for Sarah." It is a way of easing myself into words, going gently, warming up.

Write a Letter to a Writer Friend

Sometimes writing in my journal is enough to give me a jump start, and I can move directly from that to a writing project. If it is not, after I write in my journal for a while I consciously take another step toward my writing self by writing a certain kind of letter. It can't be to just anyone—it has to be to someone who knows me and cares about me as a writer, for example, my teacher/friend Elizabeth or my friend Judy who has always evoked the writer in me, although she herself is not primarily a writer. I'm not sure what to call the quality of this sort of friendship; May Sarton defined her muses as those whom she loved. Perhaps. But there are people whom I love who do not assist me to write carefully, deeply. To my brother, Sam, I would write: "Hi! How ya doin'? How are the dog shows going—get any

34

prizes lately? Shall we all get together again this Fourth of July? See ya!"
But to write to someone like Elizabeth or Judy is to write a letter as a
writer—reaching, discovering something I don't quite know, surprising
myself as I write.

If I were to write that sort of letter at this moment, it might begin like
this:

Dear Elizabeth,

*There is a fine rain falling beyond my window. It is not a pure
rain; it is mixed with blossoms it is wickedly knocking off a
tree. I have come for one delicious week to New Hampshire, to
a perfect writing retreat called A Studio of One's Own, to put
finishing touches on my new book. At home the daffodils and
forsythia have gone by, but here on this mountain it is earliest
spring.*

*A letter from Rosalie Moore Brown arrived today, in which
she has used that X-acto-knife brain of hers on my new poem,
"On a Daughter's Birthday." She sliced off the last lines, and oh,
Elizabeth, she is right! Why didn't I see it for myself? She talks in
her letter about her belief that a poet must not be too "needy" in
a poem...hmmm...I think that was not so much the problem as
my disbelief that I could trust the reader to understand what I
meant if I cut off the last few lines...*

At about that moment, I would be itching to turn to the poem and work at
revising it, trying to see what Rosalie meant and whether or not I agreed. I
would abandon my letter (poor Elizabeth!) and move solidly into my writing.

Be Ready to Stop and Turn to Your Writing Project

Often I stop midletter and turn to my writing project. But not always; I once
started a letter to a woman poet whom I did not know well, which became
52 pages of typed manuscript telling a story I had found exceptionally difficult to write in any other way. A year later it became the last section of a

new book, *Wake Up Laughing.* These friends don't know that I use them this way; they don't actually receive many letters from me, but my journal is littered with fragments beginning "Dear Elizabeth..."

Read What You Last Wrote

The moment of facing the writing task for this particular day has come. I am warmed up, I am wanting to do my work. If I am in the middle of a writing project, the first thing I do is read what I last wrote. It is best to do this reading aloud, on my feet, moving around. If you try this, let your ear hear your voice, let your feet and legs move to the rhythm of the words you have written. Read through to the very last words you wrote.

In *A Moveable Feast* Ernest Hemingway records that he made a practice of ending every day's writing at a spot where he knew what he wanted to say next. It's an excellent idea, because knowing that in five more minutes we will take a break from writing for dinner, for sleep, for an errand, we are inclined to use that five minutes to bring a feeling of closure: we "wrap up" the writing a bit. That makes getting back into the mysterious experience of writing difficult. Often what we need to do is cut the last sentence or the last paragraph from the preceding writing session before going on.

The image that comes to me is the dead wood at the tip of rosebush branches when winter is done. You look at the bush and see where the green stops and the brown, dead wood begins, and you cut off that which is dead. It's like that, coming back to a piece of writing after having "closed it down." You can tell, if you listen carefully to what you have written, where you need to cut in order to be back inside the dream, where you don't know what will happen next and everything is alive.

If You Are Not in the Middle of a Writing Project

If you are not in the middle of a writing project and need to begin something new, the process is different. You have to *begin.* Focus as precisely as you can on one detail of place or action. Don't think "novel" or "story" or

36

"poem." Think with your senses, think with your eyes, with your ears, with your sense of touch. The "open sesame" into writing is this: Capture one concrete detail. Don't worry about where it is going. Begin, as Hemingway suggests, by writing the truest sentence you know. Use your own voice. Write as if you were talking to your best friend. Grace Paley's work gives you the feeling you are listening to a funny, wise, beloved next-door neighbor on an ordinary afternoon. Look at some of the first sentences in her stories: They are clear, simple, everyday statements—the very best way to begin.

Tell me something I can't forget. Gossip. Tell the tale. There is a rich, colloquial speech that you've learned perfectly—use it. Use the power of the language you learned as a child at your own kitchen table. Your own first-learned speech is the primary color on your artist's palette. Everything else you learn will add breadth and variety, but the language of your own childhood is your greatest treasure, your primary source.

Claim Writing as Your Art Form

You do not have to make money at your writing to be a writer. Writers are artists. Although some writers make their living at their writing, most of us do not. Most of us, like artists everywhere, have other jobs on the side; we teach or work in an office or clean other people's houses or drive a truck. I no longer expect my writing to feed me or clothe me. When a small check comes in, I am delighted; I tape the attached statement onto my file cabinet; I tell my friends in workshop and we celebrate together. But even deeper is the joy I feel when my closest and keenest writing friends tell me that my writing "works," that it has reached a kind of clarity and truth, that it moves them. I want my writing to go before the world, of course. I send it out; I hope; I am pleased when it meets success among strangers. But I think I have achieved some maturity as an artist in this: What matters most to me is that I get it right for myself and for my intimate community of writers. If I am an artist, the commercial world cannot be the judge of my work. Writing is an art form that will, like every art form, take a lifetime to perfect.

You are a writer. You are an artist. Do not burden your art with the necessity of having it make your living for you. Continue to keep that possibility open if you want to, but gently. Send your work off to the best, even the most lucrative, markets first, and hope for a miracle. But remember all the famous artists who were never a commercial success; don't judge the artistic merit of your work by the fickle necessities of the marketplace.

Claiming your writing as your own personal art form is a freeing and empowering way to get started (again) and keep going.

EXERCISE 3:

Free Writing

Many authors of books on writing recommend timed, free writing as a helpful exercise to warm up, to get started (again.) In her books *Writing Down the Bones* and *Wild Mind*, Natalie Goldberg offers numerous ways of using this technique. For 10 minutes (or 5 or 15) write freely anything and everything that comes to mind. Keep your pen moving. Do not stop writing—take anything and everything that comes.

I suggest you use this exercise as a way to begin, but keep yourself free to abandon it if after one minute (or five or fifteen) you become interested in a narrative line, or an image that leans toward a poem. It is a good jump start—try it.

In the following example, written in my Tuesday workshop in Amherst, Barbara Burkart used "free," or "stream-of-consciousness," writing:

Warm-up time: keep pen on the page. Stop directing word traffic. Let it go on vacation for the night. Let new words come that I haven't used before. Censor out; time off. Freedom of fluidity of wordage and verbiage and garbage. No, I don't feel like garbage—I feel high! I immersed in my own poems today and was moved again, as I had been when I wrote them. I was thrilled to find that capacity in me to go to the core, to surrender to the magic moment when the pen starts moving on its own and I don't know where it's going but come along for the ride. It's starting...

Curvy Leverett roads shaded by pine and oak cross ancient streams. Pen moves down the road until the road stops, field starts. Get out of the car. Take off shoes, socks, tuck them neatly on the floor of the front seat. Step gingerly onto cool grass, prickly underfoot. Wildflowers brush ankles, marking their turf in pollen. Still moving. Field is shifting, descending, opening, trees are falling away. Sharp-edged crack appears in the shimmering ground, undulating under early rising sun. Shed shorts, shirt, sink ankle deep, knee deep into soft spongy earth.

Colors are changing. Lifting feet becomes burdensome; lush undergrowth beckons. Lie down. Warm shafts of light beam onto belly, shoulders. Nipples stiffen in full appreciation of the yeasty blanket that is our mother. Smile lurks, finding its way out of the corners onto well-worn wrinkled paths of flesh. Soles of the feet are getting hot, furry, like the moss under the oaks.

We can see the writer emerging as the free writing changes from her initial focus on the struggle in trying to write, to images that surprise and suggest the beginnings of a poem.

EXERCISE 4:

Remember a Photograph

A wonderful way to get started writing is to remember a snapshot or photograph. Those pictures we hold in our minds are full of emotional meaning, whether or not we consciously understand it. Remember a casual snapshot or formal photograph of yourself, and write in response to it. Or write to yourself at that age. Once, when I did this exercise, I remembered a picture of myself as an awkward teenager, my face screwed up against bright sunlight. I began a poem: "That's not my face in the photograph…" The writing took me to very strong anger and some important realization on a personal level, but it was more than a private work; the poem was later published in a literary journal.

Remember a photograph of someone close to you. You might write in first person, as in this paragraph by Dorothea Kissam, a member of my Wednesday workshop:

> I look at this picture now from my perspective of some 88 years later. My mother could not know that in four years' time she would be orphaned, her mother dead of pneumonia and her father dying within the year of drink and exposure to the New York weather.

Or you might begin writing with the words, "In this one you are…," speaking directly to the person in the photograph. I use this exercise often in my workshops, and it almost always puts a writer immediately in contact with powerful material. Paul Barrows, writing across the room from Dorothea on the same evening, began with a snapshot he remembered, and later developed the piece into a wonderful story about the relationship between two gay men.

> In this one you are looking down. You are smiling—the smile of someone who has been caught at something—a grin, a smirk— because you have just noticed me with the camera—have looked up and then looked down again—when click and buzz the shutter snaps, the film winds. In this one you are partially in shadow.

Getting started or getting started again is a matter of the spirit. Bring to your desire a gentle spirit, believing in your own stories, your own meanings. Cooperate with yourself by letting your habits and preferences work for you. And use one of the exercises in this book to get you going.

THREE

TOWARD A DISCIPLINED
WRITING LIFE

The question arises often: How can I make myself write regularly, steadily, faithfully? This is not a question of how effective the writing is but how to maintain a consistent effort.

I believe that most of what we think and read about discipline only increases writer's block. Discipline usually means making ourselves perform some duty, gritting our teeth, forcing ourselves to do what we don't want to do. A disciplined writer, we are told (or we tell ourselves) writes every day, writes X number of hours a day or X number of pages or paragraphs a day. We read how someone else structures his or her writing life, and we judge ourselves by that pattern. Unfortunately, many writing teachers reinforce this idea of discipline.

To think about writing in those ways is damaging to the creative process. I suggest a completely different approach to discipline. It has its roots in the ancient wisdom of the Hebrew prophet Zechariah: "Not by might, nor by power, but by...spirit." I suggest that the writer's way to discipline is not by mightily twisting our own arms, nor by powerfully punishing ourselves with duty and guilt, but by having a gentle, compassionate, and nonjudgmental spirit toward our own writing.

Let us look first at the challenges to discipline and then at concrete

41

suggestions for how to live a disciplined writing life.

The Challenges

The greatest challenge is to think about discipline differently. To help us do that, let us look at some of the things that keep us from our writing.

Those Other Commitments

Most of those other commitments that keep me from my writing are masks that I put up to hide my fear and my failure to do what I need and want most to do. If my belief in my own work is strong, my other commitments will adjust themselves. Human beings have free will. We have a choice. If I could speak to myself as an 18-year-old, I would say, *You can say no to the demands of your immature mother. You can insist on some privacy, some time of your own.* If I could speak to myself as a young mother of four children, I would say, *You can be writing part of the time instead of being trapped in 24-hour childcare.* Regardless of our particular circumstances, the struggle goes on to keep at one's work. If I could speak to myself just this morning when I answered the phone and the mail instead of writing, I'd say, *You can sit down, slow down, turn off the telephone.*

There is something fundamentally wrong with other commitments if they keep me from my true work. The life that is happy and makes others happy is the life that is deep and full of the joy of personal fulfillment, and personal expression is essential to personal fulfillment. The need to create is in every human being, and if that need is denied, life becomes distorted. Joseph Campbell invites you to "Follow your bliss, it never goes wrong." He is not talking about self-indulgent surface pleasures but the deepest, truest honesty to oneself; doing what one is "meant" to do. The religious tradition I grew up in talked about "call"—what Roman Catholics sometimes term "vocation." Jesus was clear about the total demand a call makes upon an individual; nothing less than abandoning everyone and everything else would do. I don't think he was talking about all the complicated systems of belief that have grown up around his sayings, but about individuation, about letting go of tradition, about claiming freedom for oneself. He was talking about the real cost of a vocation.

To be a writer or any other kind of artist is to be a person with a *vocation;* with a *call;* with *a bliss.* Art that matters is a life-and-death affair. If my child is hit by a car, I don't need a single second to decide about my priorities. I instantly abandon all the commitments I have for that day, and I take her to the hospital. Similarly, if I truly believe in my own writing, in its importance, in its value, I do not have a problem of priorities.

Belief, Not Discipline

After almost 50 years of writing and 15 years of helping other people write by leading creative writing workshops, I am convinced that the problem of discipline is lodged in the emotions, in a pattern of attitudes toward oneself and toward the idea of being a writer. The problem is not a flaw of character, that *I am just not a disciplined person.* Often those suffering from a lack of what is called discipline in writing practice are incredibly disciplined in other aspects of life. Nor does failure to be disciplined mean you are not a serious writer.

I truly despise the phrase *not a serious writer.* Often this is said by writers and writing teachers referring to someone whose work they don't like, who has paid money to take a course, rearranged her or his schedule, made a public statement by appearing in a room for a writing course. What in the world is meant by "a serious writer"? Anyone who cares enough to take a course or a workshop is *serious.* There is no place for this kind of arrogance. The desire to write is serious.

Recently I held an all-day writing workshop, and one woman, Claire MacMaster, came from the coast of Massachusetts, a four-hour round-trip, to take the workshop for that one day. As she wrote, it was clear that she was very discouraged about her writing, primarily because she had not been able to find others to read what she wrote and to share their writing with her. She had hoped to join one of my weekly workshops, but at the end of the day she told me that she could not do that; it was unrealistic, it was too far. But some of the words she wrote lingered in my mind: "*Take off your shoes and wrap yourself up in your thinking being and go write it out in the sand....Keep your hand moving or write with your toes—you are published until the tide comes in...*"

Claire is a serious writer.

How do serious writers—and we are all serious writers—keep going, keep working, keep writing, when the tide of disbelief, discouragement, loneliness keeps coming in and coming in?

The problem is not discipline. It is belief.

The Ghost of Criticism Past and Present

Teresa Pfeifer is a young woman in my workshop for women in public housing projects. She told me when she first came that she could not write. She took out of her jeans a worn letter that she had carried in a billfold in her pocket *for 17 years,* and told me this story, which she later wrote as follows:

Once, in high school, I sent a sample of my adolescent poems to a famous author of children's books that I had loved. She responded with a letter loaded with sarcasm—"It's as though you'd been frightened by a deodorant commercial," she wrote. And asked why didn't I try writing in iambic pentameter as many words as I could think of that rhymed with shit.

Looking back on these poems now, I see that I was a teenager with very sharp instincts and a hypersensitivity to the world around me which led to poems of great exaggeration (probably the gift of all teenagers in turmoil). Her responses were so cruel and without humanity that she could have just defecated on the poems and saved herself some typing. She molested my soul and I would carry the scars for years. I had nothing of value to write, I had nothing of value to say, I had nothing of value to contribute. I felt as though my psyche had been raped.

44

I urged Teresa to find those poems and show them to me. She did, and I wrote a different response to the very beautiful and passionate poems of that young girl. I told her, among other things, that her youthful poems were far better than my own had been at that age, that there was brilliance in them. She gave me the famous writer's letter and said, "I don't need this anymore." Due in part to the support she received from other women in the workshop, Teresa graduated *summa cum laude* from college and is now enrolled in the MFA program in creative writing at the University of Massachusetts, teaching undergraduate students how to write.

What Teresa did in fact, we all do in spirit. We keep the ugly words of put-down and ridicule, the discouraging grades in elementary and high school; we carry them close to us, and we use them as evidence when we say, "I can't write."

Sue Solomont joined my workshop after a period of writer's block, but she had already published in literary journals and had written a considerable amount of poetry in the context of academic workshops as she completed her Ph.D. I encouraged Sue to experiment, to trust her own voice, to "play." Her writing began to change, both in form and in subject matter; she began to write with a wild and very original imagination. After some time, having accumulated a significant number of new poems, she sent some of her new work to a former professor, among them this:

> mother mother
> buried in father
> where are U where are U
>
> voice in a snake
> yr fetal heart
> pounds through the dead king's veins
>
> in utero in the darkness of castles
> yr words lost in grandpa's grumbling
> long long table speeches

45

napkin under chin
yr fillings are wedged
you're stuffed with truffles

babies are jammed
into your heart

down my thoughts
yr thoughts echo like a

did i really hear a
        voice just then / what

wasit wasit   woke me up

did i hear weeping   in the drains

why does my heart
ache like stones
when i pour the tea &
pass the scones

Sue's voice is unique, as is her style. I found her poems fresh and interesting and very much about being a woman. But her professor responded with alarm. He said that her new work "lacked discipline."

Thomas Wentworth Higginson said the same in response to Emily Dickinson's poetry.

There are so many voices within us and outside us that discourage and undermine us, tempt us to abandon our own visions, our own voices, that a sense of duty, of "ought" and "should" will not be sufficient to counter them. The only way for me to lead a disciplined writing life is to believe in myself as a writer and to love my work so much that nothing can take it away from me. Eleanor Roosevelt insisted, "Nobody can do anything to me that I'm not already doing to myself."

Writing About Yourself

In the years I have been writing and teaching writing, I have seen many people blocked by their reluctance to write about their own lives. Gustave Flaubert expressed it best: "One does not choose one's subject matter, one submits to it." There is a sense in which the creative artist must take what comes up from the unconscious. In the tale of Bluebeard, it is the closet full of secrets that brings tragedy. The secret we try to lock away gets larger and larger, tempts us more and more, until we must open the door or die as an artist.

Meeting Your Needs as a Writer

In earlier sections of this book I have discussed the importance of knowing your own habits, rituals, patterns. Everyone's patterns are different. Discipline begins by understanding how you yourself work.

You can learn something about how you work by remembering successes of the past. For example, when you accomplished a project (fixing your car, making a garment), how did you go about it? Did you lay careful plans first and proceed in an orderly way, cleaning up after yourself as you went along? Or did you barge in with more energy than planning, change your plans as you went along, decide to do a portion of it somewhat differently from the instructions printed in the manual or on the pattern?

When you did your best writing in school (regardless of the grade it received), how did you go about writing it? Did you write daily, and finish it well before the deadline? Or were you one of those students who waited until the last two days, went without sleep, wrote around the clock, and turned in, nevertheless, a very good paper? Look at the way you worked when you did your *best* work. Which kind of person are you?

When you have begun to identify your patterns, don't berate yourself because your patterns are not like someone else's. Be realistic about the way your best work is done and cooperate with yourself.

If you like to get up early for the fresh, clear silence of dawn, make yourself coffee, and start your writing, then go to bed early enough to establish that pattern. If you like to work far into the night, when even the birds are silent, then allow yourself to sleep late enough in the morning, or take an afternoon nap, or whatever it takes so you can stay up and write.

There are those who advise, "Write at least 30 minutes each day." There are those who say, "Write for many hours, but come out of it with only one or two pages." These directions are absurd when they are given as rules applicable for all writers.

I can write four hours a day, but I cannot write 30 minutes a day. (The one exception is writing for 30 minutes in a supportive writing workshop, as described in Part Two of this book.) I have to forgive myself when there are days of no writing at all and give myself the long blocks of time that are absolutely sacred to my concentration. I cannot jerk myself out of my ordinary occupations into writing and then jerk myself back again. I must block out time in segments of four or more hours at once. Furthermore, I need to go away to a private place at least twice a year where I talk to no one and work on a major project. Later in this chapter, in the section entitled "Never Underestimate the Power of Sleep," there is more about this important possibility.

Writing by "Committee"

To lead a disciplined writing life, one must be as free as possible from all committee opinions. To write in a context of external judgment, conflict, hostility, and interruption is absurd.

An extreme example of the negative effect of writing for a committee is the experience many people have in writing traditional academic theses and doctoral dissertations. In the February 1992 issue of *College Composition and Communication,* Nancy Sommers, Associate Director of the Expository Writing Program at Harvard, gives an eloquent plea for traditional academic papers to make room for what she calls "the personal essay":

> Given the opportunity to speak their own authority as writers,
> given a turn in the conversation, students can claim their stories
> as primary source material and transform their experiences into

evidence. They might, if given enough encouragement, be empowered not to serve the academy and accommodate it, not to write in the persona of Everystudent, but rather to write essays that will change the academy. When we create opportunities for something to happen between the drafts, when we create writing exercises that allow students to work with sources of their own that can complicate and enrich their primary sources, they will find new ways to write scholarly essays that are exploratory, thoughtful, and reflective.

I want my students to know what writers know—to know something no researchers could ever find out no matter how many times they pin my students to the table, no matter how many protocols they tape. I want my students to know how to bring their life and their writing together.

Unfortunately, Nancy Sommers is still an exception rather than the rule. I have experienced so many writers coming to my workshops damaged by their experiences of writing academic papers that I feel the issue needs to be addressed.

When I was newly out of graduate school, I worked for a time editing dissertations. One was written by a foreign student preparing to return to a Third World country. His degree was to come from two departments simultaneously: chemistry and forestry. Each department had separate guidelines for the dissertation. Each had its own accepted terminology. Committee members were at odds with one another. What one professor liked, the other hated. The pawn in the whole game was the hapless student. Over and over again in the text I encountered statements like this: "The presence of a mobile abiotic transport agency which can exacerbate ecological impacts is one such example of the contribution of substrate qualities to differing seasonal impacts relative to proposed management actions." The phrase *a mobile abiotic transport agency* was used so frequently, I asked the student if he would please tell me in other words what it meant. He looked at me with surprise and said, "It means *water*." The

intense jargon made every sentence almost unintelligible, and his committee had sent him to me to assist him with the very problem I felt they had
created. I rewrote it, sentence by sentence. When he looked at all the red
pencil marks I had put on his page he said in his heavy accent, "Oh, my poor
paper! It's bleeding to death!"

Many people wanting to write have become convinced that they cannot
because they did not succeed at writing term papers, dissertations, and theses. Sometimes it is helpful to realize that academic papers written for a
committee are akin to romance novels: It is formula writing, and the formula is absolute. If you failed to write a dissertation, it may mean you were just
too creative a writer! Joseph Campbell has written: "I think of the Ph.D. as a
very funny kind of celebration; it just proves that up to the age of 45 you
have obeyed orders and haven't done your own thing."

There is another committee we often write for: the committee in our
heads. This committee is a collection of remembered parents, teachers,
friends, acquaintances—all of whom have ideas about our writing. You may
already have become acquainted with this committee if you did Exercise 2,
"Getting Rid of Internal Critics." For me, this committee includes my dead
mother, who didn't want me to reveal that I grew up poor and spent time in
an orphanage. It includes my writing companions, writers who write alongside me in my workshops, because I care so much what they think of my
work. It includes some old friends lost when I abandoned the church, and
some new friends who might be shocked to know how religious I really still
am. It includes the editor of a small, macho review who told me that in a
manuscript of my poems, only the one about the man who killed a bear was
"of any value whatsoever." My internal committee is vast, as it is for everyone who writes. There may be the high school teacher who gave you an "F"
in English, the best friend whom you don't want to offend, the famous writer
whose work you love.

With all of this against us, how can we ever believe in our work enough
to do it with consistency and joy?

SUGGESTIONS FOR LIVING A DISCIPLINED WRITING LIFE

What follows is a different way of thinking about discipline than the white-knuckle, beat-myself-over-the-head-with-guilt-and-duty approach. To be disciplined as a writer you need a compassionate and welcoming attitude about your own work and the support of others who value and call forth your writing. A huge part of leading the disciplined writing life is having other people in your life who care about your writing, want it, believe in it, and encourage it. Part Two of this book, "Writing with Others," is all about having that essential support. But being a disciplined writer begins in your own mind.

Consider Yourself an Artist

Consider yourself an artist, and consider your task simply expressing your own vision, your own voice. You don't have to prove anything to anybody. If your Auntie Matilda doesn't like your story, that's okay. If the editor of the *Atlantic Monthly* rejects your article for publication, that's okay too. You probably wouldn't like what Aunt Matilda reads, anyway. And if you are rejected by the *Atlantic Monthly* you are in excellent company. You are an artist; you are becoming an ever more skilled and original writer. Gordon Weaver declared, "A writer is one who writes; a serious writer is one who writes as well as he [sic] can as consistently as possible and for whom writing is the most serious activity he knows. How much money, fame, or publication he gets—these are extra-literary factors."

You are working at your craft, you are learning and practicing your art. You don't have to "succeed" in anyone else's eyes or perform according to anyone else's rules. Dismiss your internal committee of critics. Tell them to go take a vacation and leave you alone. Remember that Joseph Campbell statement: "Where there is a path, it is someone else's way." Find your own path. Trust your own way.

Deal with Your Envy

Two years after I completed my graduate work in creative writing, I was in a conversation with the new head of the program who told me that she had been asked to go to a university in another state to give a reading, but for personal reasons she was uncomfortable driving on throughways. I volunteered to drive her, and did so. After her reading, we were at the home of a well-known poet for a reception. I sat listening as 15 people sipped cocktails, looked at a collection of primitive masks on the walls, and talked about famous poets. They called them by their first names, and gossiped about who was divorcing whom, who had died, who was suffering from cancer. I was a woman in my mid-40s. I still had children living at home, going to high school. I was not free to apply for a teaching position with my new MFA; my family was settled in Amherst. I had started a writing workshop independent of the university; it had grown to two workshops, and I was loving my work, excited about it. Suddenly I saw myself as a nobody, as ridiculous. I felt great pain. I was the only person in the room who was an outsider to the gossip; I was just a chauffeur for one of the insiders.

When I came home, I talked with Walker Rumble, who at the time was one of the first editors of our literary magazine, *Peregrine.* "Walker," I said, "I'll never make it. I'm kidding myself. I'm 47 years old, and I don't know anybody. Succeeding as a writer is not about how good a writer you are; it's all about connections. It's about who you know, and I don't even know how to play that game. I'll never make it."

Walker was thoughtful and quiet. He had been a professor of history and had left the academic world to work at a job that would give him time to write poetry. He was setting type in the back room of a local print shop. After a moment he said slowly, "You have the respect of your own neighborhood. The corner grocer never asked for more."

There have been a few moments in my life when I have felt with a kind of cold shock that in an instant everything was changing, that the continental plates of my internal geography were undergoing a major shift. This was one of those moments. If I tried to make a cartoon of it, I would have a bolt of lightning splitting the sky and zapping me. Walker had spoken the exact truth, and in two sentences he turned me around 180 degrees. What a lovely way to live! What a lovely way to think!

Ten years have passed since that afternoon on the steps of the building where I led my workshops. I have written. I have offered my work for publication. I have been proud when something was published, and disappointed when I got more than two rejection slips in any one day's mail. But never again have I felt that burning envy of those who know and repeat each other's names in the homes of the famous.

Deal with your envy by valuing yourself and your work where you are, here and now.

Make Your Writing Time a Reward, Not a Duty

Rather than thinking of going to your writing desk as the unpleasant work of your life, think of it as a longed-for pleasure, as a hot fudge sundae, as that which pleases you, delights you; that which you love. Writers talk about writing as a compulsion, as unavoidable, even as an addiction. Let that desire to write work for you. Let it be the joy, the bliss, the call, the vocation. Let it be your reward rather than your duty.

At the end of her novel *Raw Silk*, Janet Burroway has this paragraph, spoken by a woman. I think a similar statement would be as true for many men:

> Of the three great options for fulfillment open to a woman, work and motherhood and ecstatic love, I have work left. The thing I have left is design, I haven't given that away. And I am going to approach that, work, from a new perspective....There will be space, flight, and a flow of convoluted rivers.

And Marge Piercy has written, "I belong to nothing but my work carried like a prayer rug on my back." How *do* we do this? It is a matter of love. If I am an artist, I have a vocation. As one drawn to a lover or called to a religious mission, I will go to my work because even in the hard times it is essential to my happiness.

To lead a disciplined writing life, I must love my work and believe in it. I must not allow "duty" and "ought" to be whips that drive me.

Confront the Hard Times Head On

"Writing is bull labor," one of my writing teachers said. What about the times when you hate the very thing you love? What about the times when you want to quit, take up farming or ditch digging or basket weaving? What if you decide you don't want to do it anymore?

Well, quit. Quit if you can. Entirely, I mean. Give it up. Find another art form. If it is more than you can bear, don't bear it. Sometimes a great love ends in divorce.

But if you can't quit, keep on. Love is deeper than hate. Anyone who has lived in a longtime relationship knows the truth of that statement. The harder it is, the deeper it carves you, the more love you have.

Whatever you do, don't stay in the never-never land of wanting and not doing. It will make your soul sick. If you want to write, claim for yourself what you need in order to learn, grow, practice. There is no other way to be an artist.

Put Your Writing First

The world does crowd in. Not only do our other commitments nibble at our concentration, but other forms of artistic expression may distract us. It occurred to me one day that my mother was at heart an artist. She made things like quilts. She crocheted tablecloths. She made children's clothes and Christmas ornaments and embroidered wall hangings. Sometimes she wrote. A little bit. She did a lot of different things, a little bit. At the moment I recognized this about my mother, I myself was standing beside my sewing machine planning to piece a quilt—a project that would consume hundreds of hours of concentrated time.

Suddenly I saw that I had to make a choice. I said to myself, "You can't have it all." You can't parent four children and crochet and preserve jellies and make quilts and also write. The other forms of personal expression are things I truly like to do, but that day I stopped practicing those other forms forever, because I wanted most to be a writer. I wanted to be an artist. And I knew I would have to be faithful to the practice of my art. That was when I set up an office for myself in half a basement room and began (again) to write. (Although, I admit, I do still sometimes bake bread!)

Never Underestimate the Power of Sleep

Leading a disciplined writing life is not all about work. It is also about sleep. Entering and staying in the mysterious place from which writing comes requires an engagement of the unconscious mind.

I had been blocked for two years at the exact middle of my first novel when it occurred to me to go away for one week, read without interruption the 150 pages I had completed, and sleep. It worked. On the third day I woke lying flat on my back with my manuscript on my belly and the end of the novel in my mind.

Sleep can be crucial to the completion of larger works, crucial to finding your way into (or back into) your writing when you are distant from it. When you are blocked or extremely scattered, busy in a life of making your living, fulfilling your obligations, sleep can be the *open sesame* back into your art. Whatever you may think of the popular notions of giving oneself subliminal suggestions, or asking the mind to solve problems in sleep, there is some wisdom in acknowledging that the unconscious mind will either help or sabotage creative work. The unconscious mind will not be manipulated or coerced, but it must be *engaged* for our work to be all that it can be.

When you are exhausted, as after weeks of intense or scattered work, it takes three days and nights of sleep for the "tapes" in your head to slow down. By that, I mean the voices that go on and on in your mind. "Don't forget that memo that has to be typed tomorrow. Don't forget to pick up a new contact lens before the shop closes on Saturday. Why doesn't Doris leave that bastard?" In religious retreat circles, there is talk of the "deep silence" that begins on the third day. The first time I went on a silent retreat, I slept most of the time (off and on, but more sleeping than waking) until the third day, when I woke up with a startled sense that something was different. There was silence *inside* me, as well as outside me. This may sound scary, but it isn't. It is peaceful like no other peace I have felt in my life. It feels like a new beginning, like the first line of a hymn from an old Presbyterian hymnal: *Morning has broken, like the first morning; blackbird has spoken, like the first bird...*

Sleep is one of the primary reasons why I recommend going away by yourself for a while. You need to be where you can go in and out of sleep, waking, dreaming, floating half between sleep and consciousness, but on a dedicated journey with a very specific purpose in mind: to get from where you are to the secret that lies at the heart of your writing. Do not make of sleep another "should" or "ought." Just allow sleep to come and go as a good friend, when it wants. Keep no schedule. Eat only when you are hungry. If you wake, read or walk, then welcome sleeping when it returns, and consciously desire the resting and sorting out of images in your mind that will help you in your writing.

My favorite places are near the ocean, and poet Ann Stokes's retreat in New Hampshire. (See Ann's poem at the end of the section titled "On Unrhymed Poetry" in Chapter Six.) In most areas of the country there are special writing retreats. You can get information on many of these from *Poets and Writers*, 72 Spring Street, New York, NY 10012.

In the first three days of solitude I do not allow myself to do anything out of duty. I do exactly as I please: I read, sleep, walk along the shore, sleep, daydream, sleep, all the while knowing I am gently, gently going toward my writing. I cannot stress strongly enough how important I feel this is, especially when you are dealing with a block in your writing. It is wonderful; it is magical; it is an act of trust in your own unconscious to assist you when the conscious mind is too weary or too tangled with anxiety. And it works. Best of all, for me, is sleeping where I can hear the sound of surf. It is as if my mind is being washed clean of distractions and I am allowing myself to go into the ocean of my own unconscious, where I am connected to everything and everyone, and anything is possible.

I confess that if I had read this when I was a young mother I would probably have said, "What luxury she is talking about! Days alone by the ocean! Sure! And where will I get the money to do something like that?" Now, looking back, I feel sad that I did not provide for myself regular times alone. I could have done something. We were poor, it is true, but I could have found a way if it had seemed as important as I now know it was. Off-season rates at country inns, private rooms at religious retreat centers, bed-and-breakfast houses, the summer place of a friend, a tent in the woods and a manual typewriter—there are many possibilities. What I lacked was belief in myself, in the importance of my writing, in my own gifts. I was unable to put my writing before all of my other commitments. I was unable to insist that others in my life help me to have time apart, time alone.

To go away alone is one of my patterns, my needs. I do not suggest that it is right for everyone, but there are habits and patterns which are right for you. Only you can know what those are, claim them, welcome them, cooperate with your own unconscious.

When All Else Fails

All of the above is about the subjective, inner condition of the psyche, where I believe the problem of discipline hides. However, I must admit that there are times when I hit myself over the head with a big stick. When all of my subjective wisdom fails to get my attention, as sometimes it does, I have a gimmick for getting really tough on myself. Like everything else, it works because it fits my particular personality. I was the kind of student who waited until the last screaming minute to write a term paper, then stayed up all night and did an excellent job. I work well under pressure. Since I know that about myself, occasionally I play a trick on myself by setting up a deadline that functions for me like an old school assignment used to function. I call my agent in New York City and promise her a manuscript in a certain number of weeks. Then my pride and my unwillingness to fail start to bug me. The manuscript I have promised begins to talk to me: Give me time! Give me time! Look at the calendar! Give me time! Calling my agent works because losing her respect is a serious threat. I have never yet failed to meet a deadline I myself have announced to her. A deadline only works if I am going to suffer by not meeting it. Telling my best friend is not a deadline —she doesn't really care whether I meet it or not.

Some writers in my workshops use this technique, tell us when to expect a manuscript, and if it does not appear on schedule, we ask for it publicly and express disappointment. Others say this would only cause them to feel blocked; it would apply a pressure that would be counterproductive. Know your own habits, let them work to assist you.

Do Not Judge Your Work

William Stafford's statement "What one has written is not to be defended or valued, but abandoned: others must decide significance and value" might well be printed on a three-by-five card above most writers' desks. When you have done all you can do, when you have written and revised and brought to your work the finest craft of which you are capable, your job is to let it go. It is like raising a child—the parent cannot hold on forever.

I know a woman who has been in many writing workshops over many years, always working on one short story. Recently someone said to me, "I saw Lucille the other day. Hadn't seen her for ages. She's still working on the story about the beaver." We all know the feeling of frustration in wanting our work to be more perfect than it is, but there comes a time when we must let it go. W. H. Auden once remarked that only four poems in any book he published were ever finished. All the rest, he said, he gave up on. After I had worked on a black gospel musical for two years in Maury Yeston's musical theater workshop at BMI in New York City, Maury suddenly stopped giving me the encouragement I had been enjoying, told me it was time to consider it finished and said, "Get to work on another project." It was good advice. Take your writing as far as you can take it, then send it out into the world. Let it go.

And yet, the final authority can never be someone else telling you how to write, or what to write, or whether you have done it well, or when the time has come for you to consider it finished. It is your art. Listen to the reactions of others. Learn from them. But the bottom line, the last word, is this: It is yours. Your art. You will be disciplined when you are free and in love with your art. Martha Graham, speaking to dancers, could have been speaking to any artist, any writer: "There is a vitality, a life force, an energy, a quickening which is translated through you into action, and because there is only one of you in all time, this expression is unique. And if you block it, it will never exist."

ON KEEPING A JOURNAL

Most popular approaches to journal keeping stress personal therapy; some emphasize daily recording of events as a way to write an autobiography for one's descendants. A writer's journal can be these things, but it can be more.

In his excellent book *Dream Work,* Jeremy Taylor encourages people to use all the available methods for dream interpretation, because each has something to offer, but no one is sufficient alone. He says dreams are like holograms, with many sides, many simultaneous meanings. My approach to the writer's journal is similar. Outside your own person, your journal is your single most important asset. It can surely be the place where you record daily events or work through personal matters, but as writer/artist, it is your mulch, your seedbed, the womb of your art. It can be the safe place for writing first-draft material, for experimenting, for gathering and keeping impressions and information for future work.

As the sketchbook is to the artist, so the journal is to the writer. In the sketchbook, a finger does not have to be connected by a full body to a toe. Visual artists sketch, but people who write often seem to require of themselves that every word which drips off the pen should be "Literature." Writers need a place where the single interesting line can lie dormant waiting for the novel that is germinating in it. In 1980 I sang a little ditty in my mind and wrote it in my journal, and for some reason it would not go away. *It was August of the year that Augie died. Marigolds and miracles bloomed side with horny-toads.*

Now, I ask you: Who would think anything would come of that? But after three years of carrying it around in my head, one day I asked myself, *Who is Augie?* It was as if I had turned around in my mind and looked directly at something that had been at the periphery of my consciousness. And there stood Augie. He was a veteran of the Korean War, a vagrant, a drifter who killed himself one day in a back room of a farmhouse. Augie was fiction (that is, he was a collage of imagined and lived images), and my novel, *If That Mockingbird Don't Sing,* was born.

My journal is the seedbed for everything I write, the place where no judgment applies, not even my own. In order to write clearly, I have to think clearly. Working on my writing is in a profound sense working on myself. Everything I come to understand about myself is a deepening of the potential for my own writing, because it is an increase in wisdom, in understanding, and in the possibility of empathy, without which no writing can ever be great. My daughter Laurel said to me one day, "The distance you can take other people is the distance you have traveled yourself."

What does a journal look like? My friend Sharleen Kapp argued with me once in a workshop when I was waxing ecstatic about the merits of journal keeping. "I don't keep a journal," she stated. But Sharleen never leaves home without a bound book of blank pages; all of her first-draft writing in workshop is done in these books, and when she is not writing, she sketches in them.

I teased her, "Sharleen, what are those books?"

"I don't know..." She hesitated. "But they're not a journal."

A journal can be anything, or look like anything, that helps you. You don't have to call it a journal. Often, the blank book, or notebook, or journal, or sketchbook is the best place to work through your own feelings about your writing. Donna Bashaw, a writer new to my workshop, somewhat over-whelmed by the variety of exercises and the writings of others she was hearing around her, followed my suggestion that she write about her feelings in her journal. She wrote the following:

With every new suggestion, sharp images quicken my pulse—words anxious for display.

I imagine them like brush strokes of a painter—simmering in the corners of some remote part of the mind—known to the painter long before they're seen and tangible to the world.

How many stories and poems and paragraphs are lurking within me? Will they ever run out? How can I possibly ever hope to write down all that I need and want to say? The years spent without a pen as my friend. The happiness, fear, anger, hope and despair—silenced—unspoken—invalidated. Untold stacks of the unsaid, unwritten.

I want all that isn't writing to become secondary to writing. I want my words to become real, my thoughts carved. I am impatient with all the other people I must be. I want to make up for time lost. I want to write pages about every image. Nothing else will satisfy me. Indulge in obsessive writing—indulge in my craft.

I feel as though the little I've seen of my writing is the surface of a deeper chasm. I want to know what's in there. I want to go further than the fear, past the pain. I want my hand to become one with my pen.

As we talked about what she had written, it became clear to Donna that what was frightening her was not so much what she was hearing from outside herself as the pressure of rich possibilities within herself—all that wanted to come forth in her writing.

WHY DOES KEEPING A JOURNAL HELP A WRITER?

Remember my friend whose husband said, "You sit there writing as if your life had some significance"?

Why do it? Why write in a journal?

Because your life has significance.

61

It Can Be Closest to Your Natural Speech

A journal is private. It is safe. It is a place where language can flow free of editors, critics, teachers, and well-meaning but ruinous relatives and friends. In a journal, thought and feeling can come together without self-consciousness. I learn more about the true voice of a writer when he or she is reading a journal entry than I do in countless attempts at some form, because the root of writing is our own speech. In her book *The Poet in the World,* Denise Levertov believes "notebooks to be perhaps the only sure and honest way a writer can stimulate his [sic] creativity—that is, find out that he has more to write than he thought, as distinct from forcing himself to write when he has nothing to say." It is in a journal that many writers take the risk of honesty for the first time.

It Reveals the Way You Think

If you write daily, you catch yourself in the act of your own mental habits. The bad habits become boring. "Nice day today" becomes singularly uninteresting by the 14th day, and if you want to practice your writing, you may be moved to more concrete language. "I'll tell you how the sun rose—a ribbon at a time..." begins Emily Dickinson's evocation of one beautiful day. The hardest thing ever said to me as a writer—hardest to hear, hardest to deal with—was my teacher Andrew Fetler's pronouncement soon after I began studying with him: "The problem is not with the way you write; it's with the way you *think*." It took me years to admit that the thinking he saw in my writing was my *received thinking,* not my deepest, raw, vulnerable (original) thinking. I tell this story in Part Two of this book, "Writing with Others."

It Helps You Remember

The title of Judith Moore's essay "Save Your Life: Notes on the Value of Keeping a Diary" is at the heart of the matter. A diary, a journal, does save the perception you have of this day as you are living it. If that matters to you, then the keeping of a daily log, a diary, a journal of remembrance, is valuable. The little five-year diary I kept between ages 10 and 15 would not tell much of consequence to another reader, but for me it contains coded references to the year and a half I spent in an orphanage, the painful circumstances that put me there, and the trauma of coming back home. What is valuable to me is the voice of the child I was, the necessity I felt even then of protecting family secrets, hiding the truth that seemed shameful. The journal I kept all through college (the word "diary" seemed childish to me then) is difficult for me to read now, because it reveals to me my fundamentalist passion in that time of my life, my narrow and fearful view of religious experience. As I write these words, however, I am struck by the importance of going back and dealing with that part of my history.

Whether or not we have saved our lives in journals, everything we have experienced is recorded in our conscious or unconscious minds, and it is not too late to begin to write that rich material now. Bob Burton was in my workshop at the Graduate Theological Union in Berkeley during the winter of the 50th anniversary of Pearl Harbor. As a young man, he had been on one of the ships closest to Bikini Atoll when the first atomic bomb was detonated there. Bob's account of his experience, written in workshop, is a journal entry 45 years after the event:

> The TV commentary said, "America's most horrendous action....I'm guilty and bear some of the sins for what happened then....Remembering back to 1946—
> We were steaming 7-12 miles off Bikini—the shipboard command came—"About Face"—"Put your heads down"—"Cover your eyes with your forearms"—(Officers had special glasses to see the blast)—WHOMMmmm
> The command "About face"—
> The mushroom cloud—
> Wow!!!!
> Later—"Let's hit the beach, Gootch"—
> "Ain't any Bikini Atoll left at all" he said—
> "Gootch, they wouldn't let us go ashore if there wasn't any beach"—

Broken beer bottles and dead fish—
Coral Reef Shack Tavern gone—
Had to clean up the beach before we could play baseball—
Gootch bet a couple of beers he could throw a baseball across
the atoll—stood ankle deep in water and threw—ball splashed at
water's edge on other side—as easy as a flea could jump from skin
to skin across the cloth material in a bikini bathing suit....
Brushed the sawdust off our warm beers—clicked the bottles
together—Gootch offered the toast—"Here's looking up your old
address"—
— belch—

In light of what we now know, Bob's words are a powerful evocation of the
ignorance and—yes—innocence of the young sailors and their officers
whose special glasses were supposed to protect them from the terrible thing
that was unleashed that day. It helps me, as well as Bob, to remember and to
try to understand.

It Is Context for Healing and Growth

Everything we have experienced is kept by our minds, and even if we do not
remember on the conscious level, old events can block us as writers and
inhibit growth as persons. The journal is one place where we can invite
secrets to reveal themselves when we are ready to see, ready to remember.
Understanding where we came from can help us heal the wounds of the
past and therefore live more freely and powerfully in the present.
According to Kierkegaard, "Life can only be understood backwards, but it
must be lived forwards."

WHAT MIGHT A JOURNAL CONTAIN?

A journal may contain anything. It is personal to you and may be as simple
or as complex as you choose. What follows are suggestions that you can

incorporate as a working plan for a journal or simply to open up possibilities. I use all of these, but not in any structured way.

A Daily Log

Be gentle with yourself. Let the journal be an invitation, not a duty. When you have missed a day, or many days, jot your remembrance of them if you want to. Don't set a required amount of writing to be done each day. On some days one friend of mine just writes, "I'm here." Write concretely, specifically. Not just a bird, but a fledgling finch that hasn't got its red feathers yet and bares its speckled breast as it lifts its head to receive nourishment. (And don't be daunted by what you don't know; pictures of finches are in every North American field guide to the birds.) Use words that enable you to see, taste, touch, hear, smell. Deal with inner feelings as well as external events. Express your anger; use four-letter words if they are natural to you. Free yourself to change the subject, to scratch out, to cuss, to pray, to contradict yourself. If Walt Whitman can do it, so can you: "They say I contradict myself. All right, I contradict myself."

Sketches and Vignettes

Flights of fancy. Philosophical wanderings. Memories. Bits or long stretches of pure, detailed description. When I go back to my journal, some of the passages that give me most pleasure are descriptions of simple, daily occurrences: a squirrel on a wooden fence outside my study window; how the rain made dark patterns on the light-gray bark of a winter maple. These are writing practices, but they are also resources for short stories and poems, and a way of remembering days otherwise lost.

Suggestions for Using Sketches and Vignettes

1. Allow images to float to the surface.

This exercise comes from Ira Progoff, whose Intensive Journal Workshops and book *The Intensive Journal* have been helpful to many people. Imagine yourself looking down into a deep well. You are safe, comfortable, looking over the edge and down. You can see the surface of water, far, far down. As you watch the water, allow images to rise up to the surface and float there, then recede again below the surface as other images rise. Do this as long as you want, then write whatever comes to you to write.

2. Light a candle, turn off the lights, listen to music, and write.

Allow yourself to relax, and invite memories. Allow your inner eye to see, your inner ear to hear. Then write whatever comes to you to write. I had done this for years before I heard that the Proprioceptive Writing Workshops use this technique and recommend Baroque music as particularly evocative. I have found that music that evokes the listener's own childhood or young adulthood can be effective. Recorded sounds of nature—rain, the sea, woodland birds, wild wolves—are also good resources.

3. Take your journal to a fast-food place and jot down fragments of conversation.

Later, develop those fragments into a dialogue between imagined characters. There is an example of this technique in Chapter Five, "Finding Your Voice and Using Other Voices."

Letters

My friend, children's book writer Jane Yolen, has had difficulty keeping a journal because of reasons related to privacy, what she calls "ineptness at writing by hand," and distrust of writing on a project she fears will never be published. In an article in the *Daily Hampshire Gazette* she wrote humorously of her own repeatedly broken New Year's resolutions to write in her journal. "But I think I have solved the problem at last," she says. "I have taken to writing my journal as a letter to interested friends which I compose on a typewriter. The whole thing is kept in file folders afterward. I have been going solidly for seven months now."

Letters are a wonderful way to begin writing (again), especially those

66

written to people who stimulate the writer in you. As I said earlier, after a time away from my writing I almost always begin with a journal entry and a letter, moving from that to the writing project I am currently trying to complete.

Suggestions for Using the Letter Form in Your Journal

1. Write a letter to a friend.

Sometimes the letter form is helpful beyond being a jump start. A few years ago I was traveling to Europe for the first time in my life, and I would be spending eight days alone in Italy. My friend and mentor, Elizabeth Berryhill, said to me, "I will never go there. Be my eyes. See it for me." During those eight days, I wrote over a hundred handwritten pages of journal, being Elizabeth's eyes and ears in the great museums of Florence, standing before Michelangelo's *David* and climbing the ancient, narrow steps of the Duomo.

I learned in those days how to write description. I had never before wanted so badly to give to my reader all that my eyes saw, all that my tongue tasted. Letters that call from you your best writing are your art. Emily Dickinson's letters are treasures. She wrote and rewrote them. She was practicing her art.

2. Write a letter you don't intend to mail.

Write to the person you didn't marry, or to someone else significant to you who is no longer in your life, or to someone who is in your life, saying things you don't want them to hear. This can help to break down writing blocks. The things we need to say but cannot say often are the foundation stones of our resistance to writing.

The example that follows was written by Connie Bryon. It is a letter to her mother, not intended to be mailed.

I have a different way of looking at it. Does it surprise you? Did you know I'm not you? If you want me to tell your story you have to let me tell it my way. You can't ask me to tell your story and then tell me how to tell it. You can't have it all.

You weren't the worst mother in the world. But you weren't perfect either, and if I tell your story, you will be human as you are. With your strengths and weaknesses, foibles and shortcomings. All that will be on the line like the Gypsy wash you warned me about.

Our lives were like the clothes on the line—hung a certain way for the neighbors, sheets first, then pillowcases hiding the underpants hung by size, then undershirts, blouses, skirts, and dresses all hung upside-down by the hems, towels, large ones first, then hand towels and face cloths, pulled taut without sagging middles since clothesline was something we had plenty of.

You can tell a lot about a family by the clothes on the line, and hanging clothes out is a dying art. Now I rarely do it, but when I do I still find myself draping the damp items over the edge of the basket. My basket is yellow plastic, but I can clearly see the old wooden bushel baskets we used. And here I am, still sorting the clothes before I hang them so I can match the items, hang the socks by the pair, and always announce to the viewers there is no chaos in this house. Everything is as it should be, everything is in its place.

If I tell your story, it will not be like that clothesline so neat and artificially proper. Your story is about a real woman, proud to a fault. Don't tell anyone your name is on the school's Indigent Book List, you said. Don't tell anyone your father is a drunk, your parents are divorced. Don't tell the family secrets, you said. Now you want me to tell it your way. Mom, you can't have it both ways.

3. Write a letter to a center of power: to God, to the world, to your boss, to some power that pleases or oppresses you.

Get things off your chest by letting your language express how you feel about the way things are.

4. Write a letter to improve the world or to help someone, and mail it!

Write to the president or your congressional representative or someone else who works on your behalf. Most of us underestimate our own power, the difference we can make by complaining or thanking those who need to know our opinions. I keep copies of letters I mail to persons in government, as a record of things about which I feel strongly.

Write to the owner of the gas station where a nice young man helped you when you couldn't get the self-service pump to work. A writer in my workshop did this, and months later got a letter back from Ethiopia, the young man's mother expressing gratitude because that letter earned her son a promotion in a foreign land. Recommend a promotion—you could improve the world for someone else!

5. Write a letter to yourself at a younger or older age.

You might make it a love letter, give yourself some appreciation. Or write to the writer in you, and allow the writer to answer. You may be surprised! Virginia Woolf, after reading something she had written when she was young, wrote in her diary, "My! How that young woman could write!"

6. Write to a part of yourself you have left behind, or to the self you might have been if you had made different choices in your life.

After having a series of disturbing dreams set in the inner-city slum street where I grew up, I went to a Jungian therapist to work on my dreams. She advised, "You left a part of yourself on Olive Street in St. Louis; it is going to keep coming back until you go back there and reclaim it." I have written a play, *Berries Red,* in which the adult narrator goes back and talks to the child she used to be. And I allowed the child to answer, in all her rage. It was a profoundly healing writing experience. And in performance, it was my best play.

7. Write a letter in response to something that makes you laugh.

After I handed out the "Swopper's Column" from the October 1992 *Yankee Magazine* in my workshop, Barbara Hales responded to this item: "Will swop complete set of *Yankee* from January 1976 to present for English Springer Spaniel memorabilia."

> Dear Sir,
> Unfortunately I have disposed of more than seven Hefty bags full of spaniel head curls and foot feathers. Would you like pictures of eight very fat, very tiny pups one by one learning to tumble out of their whiskey crate carrying box?
>
> Or would you like soft and coarse brushes; a flea comb; hair spray; flea spray; special shampoo for white coat; special shampoo for black coat; special shampoo for fleas?
>
> Maybe you would like a rusty choke collar; a mildewed leather collar; a show leash; a frayed 30-foot tracking leash. Or maybe you would prefer a dumbbell, and a bona fide Companion Dog certificate with a pewter bust of a spaniel to go with it? Yes, you read right, a pewter bust on a maple plaque.
>
> It breaks my heart, but I want those Yankee Magazines really badly...

Writing in response to want ads may take you to a serious place. Louise Podkowka wrote the following piece about how she decided to join my workshop:

> Ordinary. Barbara Jane was ordinary. She scanned the Sunday paper for a place to go and found the Community Calendar. A full page of things to do today. As she made her way down the list, her doubts began to grow. Singles, Overeaters, Debtors, Narcotics, Birthparents, Lesbians, Divorce, Crossovers, Toughlove. Group after group excluded her; Gamblers, Abused Women, Survivors. Barbara Jane didn't fit in, and she thanked the stars that came out

at night that she was just ordinary. She couldn't help but wonder what had gone wrong—or was it right?—with her life to be excluded from the Community.

Barbara Jane combed her straight brown hair, smiled a crooked-tooth grin, and put on the cotton sleeveless dress she wore when making dinner. She pressed her face on the window, looking out for a clue, thinking there must be a place or something she'd forgotten that would make her fit in. She looked at the long list again. The Writers' Group caught her eye. Beginners, it said, were welcome. Does that mean even someone who had never written except in school because they had to? Maybe Barbara Jane could join that group, but she wondered what she'd write about; her life was a dull routine, nine-to-five job. She did read the Book-of-the-Month Club book but usually never finished it. She watched some TV at night but found it made her cry. True stories, a kidnapped child, burning bridges, burning houses, burning husbands. It was all that true stuff that scared her so.

Items You Want to Save

You may want to use your journal as a notebook, as a scrapbook. Your journal is a place to collect things of significance to your life or to your writing. Clippings, quotes (always write down your sources—author, book, page number—otherwise, when the day comes to use that wonderful saying by someone else, you will be vastly frustrated), photographs, letters from other people that impact on the story of your own life. Most writers use the events of their own lives in their fiction. A friend of mine who is a minister told me that a well-known novelist, a member of her church, asked her to have lunch with him. As they ate, he told her of the trouble in his marriage, and she counseled him. In his next novel, the protagonist's marriage was in trouble; he called his minister and over lunch they held exactly the conversation my friend had held with her parishioner. To all the world except my friend and the novelist, the vignette in the novel was pure fiction.

Drawings, Paintings, Doodles

When my daughter was in fourth grade, her teacher called me in, very upset. She had asked the children to keep a journal, and Bethany had insisted on drawing in her journal, sometimes on the same pages where she was writing. The teacher forbade it, and Bethany complied obediently for a while, then erupted into drawing a large toilet in the middle of her journal writing.

I said I thought both drawing and writing were methods Bethany uses to find out what she feels, what she wants to say. The teacher cried out in disbelief, showing me the drawing of the toilet: "Well, what in the world do you think *this* means?" I replied, "I think it means she is a very angry little girl!"

What Bethany could not say, she could draw. Use your journal freely: draw, doodle, paste—write.

Dreams

Dreams are rich sources of imagery, pure gifts from the unconscious. It is written in the Talmud: "A dream uninterpreted is a letter unopened." Write the dream and then play with it: jot down waking associations that might help you to understand it. Write a dialogue in which you speak to images from the dream, and write down what they answer.

In a difficult time when I was young, I once dreamed an image of three women. One of them was very powerful, very beautiful, and not young. I was drawn to her, fascinated by her, and wanted to know what the dream meant. Elizabeth Berryhill suggested I write a dialogue and ask the woman in the dream who she was. I did, and the woman in the dream "answered" in the words I wrote, saying that she was my own self, waiting for me to become strong. The answer surprised me and gave me strength in that difficult time.

First Drafts of Writing

Honor the raw material of first drafts. After all, it is your daydreaming; it is the history of your mind's journey. Enter it into your journal. I write all first drafts as if they are only journal entries. They may never go beyond my journal, and writing for my journal feels safe from all criticism, including my own.

Use the Media for Ideas and Responses

Begin with an item from the news, from police reports, personal ads, or swaps columns.

These are often excellent triggers for writing. Recently, in our town, which is home to three colleges, there was an item in the newspaper with the headline "Mother Climbs in Dorm Window." A national paper carried the news that "Man Keeps Dead Parents in Attic." Headlines like these are just begging to have fiction written in response. Just think of what might unfold from this want ad, which appeared recently in our local paper: "Sadie the Cleaning Lady, call Mrs. Finch." Or this notice taped to a telephone pole near the center of town: "BILL! WE KNOW YOU TOOK IT. PLEASE! RETURN IT NOW! WE WON'T GO TO THE POLICE! IT IS AN HEIRLOOM! PLEASE, BILL!"

SOME BASIC STRATEGIES FOR WORKING IN A JOURNAL

Here are some ideas for working in a journal. You will invent more as you go along—a journal invites invention.

First-Person Prose Narrative

"I went to the post office this morning, got distracted, had a bagel and read the *New York Times.* Should have been writing."

Dialogue with Your Inner Voice

"I went to the post office this morning."

"Yes, you damned fool. And then you bought the *New York Times* and went to the Classé Cafe and ate a bagel."

"So?"

"You should have been writing on your book."

"I need my exercise! Dr. Chandran said if I don't walk I'll get osteoporosis!"

    (*Sneering*) "And I suppose Dr. Chandran told you to eat that cinnamon raisin bagel slathered with cream cheese, too?"

    "Bug off!"

    "Write!"

    "All right, already!"

The dialogue form in the journal may be very fruitful when applied to an image in a dream or undertaken with a person (living or dead) with whom you have an unresolved relationship. A writer in my workshop once wrote a dialogue between herself and the man she was engaged to marry who had died in combat years before. She began by writing, "Why did you never write to me?" An answer immediately popped into her mind: "Because I write lousy letters, and I was so afraid of losing you." The answer was surprising, but she kept on with the dialogue and what emerged satisfied her. It doesn't matter whether the answer came from her own unconscious or from beyond this physical life; the result was healing.

    A dialogue doesn't have to be with a person at all; it can be with an animal, with an object, with the weather, with one's own body, with a figure in a dream. It can be with yourself—with two or more inner voices, as in my example above. Virginia Woolf considered a biography complete if it covered "six or seven of the thousand personalities" that a person might have.

Suggestions for Using Dialogue

1. Write a dialogue between yourself and someone who is no longer in your life.

Ira Progoff suggests that before you write the dialogue, you think of what he calls "stepping stones." Make a list of concrete events in the life of a significant person who is no longer in your life—your mother, for example. List one major event for each five years of her life. Listing life events is helpful because it moves the person (your mother) out of *the mother in your mind* into the context of her own life. Immediately after making that

74

list, write a dialogue with your mother.

I suggest you try this exercise at different times with and without stepping stones; there are times when doing the dialogue the other person just as he or she is imagined within yourself may be valuable.

A friend did this exercise, writing to her dead grandmother. She asked, "Grandma, why didn't you ever love me?" After writing the question, she sat silently, listening, until an answer rose up within her: "Before you were born, there was another grandchild who died, whom I loved so completely, when you came along I was afraid to love you; I didn't think I could bear it if I lost you."

The dialogue went on; at the end, my friend felt she had met her grandmother for the first time, and that she had been loved after all.

2. Write a dialogue between yourself and one of your dream images.

I did this exercise, writing a dialogue with a great, petrified tree that had fallen across my yard in a dream. Also in the dream was a young tree, and I was climbing that tree. At that time my husband and I, who had been serving churches as minister and wife for more than 20 years, were deciding to leave the church. It was a frightening time; we had no idea how we would support ourselves and our four children. Before I wrote the dialogue, the image was terrifying. I began by writing, "Tree, why did you fall?"

The answer that came into my mind and onto my page was, "Because I had gotten too big. I couldn't stand anymore."

The answer was strangely comforting. The tree continued, "Look at the young tree."

I saw myself climbing the young tree, and knew there was something new in the chaos of all that was petrified, broken, around me. My understanding of the dream shifted to an image of hope.

3. Write a dialogue between a character you are writing about and his or her lover.

Or mother. Or sister. Or father. Or...

4. Write a dialogue between yourself and yourself.

Jim Eagan, a writer in my workshop who is both carpenter and therapist, suggests doing this between the self you are now and a former self. For me, this might mean myself as I am now—a 58-year-old woman—and myself as a teenager, the sort of dialogue I actually wrote in my play *Berries Red.* For Jim, it might mean a dialogue between himself now and himself in another incarnation.

A fascinating way to do a dialogue with yourself is to write one voice of the dialogue with your right hand and the other voice with your left hand. The dominant hand accesses one side of the brain, the recessive hand accesses the other side. According to the painter Paul Klee, "The left [hand] works differently from the right. It is not so deft, and for that reason sometimes of more use to you."

Charlene Ellis, who teaches creative writing at Vermont College, suggested this technique to me and credits this exercise with changing her life. She had been very conflicted about whether or not to build a little cabin in the woods on some property she owned. For years she had dreamed of the cabin, but there were always arguments against it. She set for herself the question, "Do I want to build a cabin in which to write?" The exercise convinced her that it was essential, and she now writes in the little cabin she helped to build.

In the following example Carol Edelstein allows this exercise to lead her into a short story:

When the Left Hand Speaks with the Right

already I forgot and wrote the date with my right hand

(*already I forgot and wrote the date with my right hand*)
You dummy. I'll take that. It's good to go fast and not keep up
with my thoughts but at least be in the vicinity.

There is no vicinity like vanity

(*There is no vicinity like vanity.*)

I'm already sick of helping you. You think you can be wise with your little aphorisms. "Amphora is no tobacco," you're probably about to say, like it's so profound.

the profound is in the pond

(*The profound is in the pond.*)

I can agree with that, I thought of that myself. The pond we thought of, place where there was microscopic fresh water wriggling life, conjugation of the paramecia, and we could take turns looking at them through your father's microscope, and without being embarrassed I could stand so close to you.

close to what. The self-jelly is everywhere. The mess of the left hand is always close.

(*Close to what? The self-jelly is everywhere.*
The mess of the left hand is always close.)

He was an ugly boy by some standards—fat, and with glasses so thick since age five his eyes were like the goldfish in the greenhouse tank, like he was lost in the slimy weeds where nobody could talk to anybody else because of a rule of atmosphere—a watery medium through which words could not pass, and even the shimmer of bodies was not language, and even the grasses moving in response was not language, so how could I love him?

But I said, "Wanna go with me? Be my partner?" because we were to be in pairs, and he did not seem grateful but said yes. Then it's all blank until we are crouched by the pond with a net and a jar, and happy to know that whatever we could catch we

77

would not see yet, the jar would look empty except for the water and a bit of sludge nobody can help, but in there was the most obedient of God's creatures, multiplying, multiplying, because it was their only job.

Back up at the top of the house, where we were alone with the microscope and slides, in a little room where his mother kept her sewing machine and ironing board and a little untouchable wicker sofa that was piled high with fancy, creased tablewear from an old occasion, I saw how soft his neck was near the collar and when he removed his glasses to look through the microscope, before he knew it would be better to keep them on, for a few seconds his face was all bare, and his eyes were small and given to me like good bright berries, the way a creature, dog or kitten, even our box turtle from Fitzgerald Lake before he went behind the sofabed, could look and see I was not a girl at all but one of the shapes in the world, moving like the curtains, which were weighted at the bottom by what I liked to pretend were gold doubloons.

So I did not kiss his neck or touch his hair as I wanted to, but said, "Let me take a look...Can you see any?" and he said...

Carol's story goes on, having begun with the very internal act of writing a dialogue between her left and right hands.

Free Association

Freely write images or words as they pop into your mind. See where your mind will take you when you release control. If jingles or rhymes occur, let them come and go, do not repress or edit or manipulate. Use incomplete sentences, phrases, single words. Many writers find that setting a certain time helps: "I will not stop my pen from moving for five minutes..."

Clustering and Mapping

Gabriele Lusser Rico's book *Writing the Natural Way* has many suggestions for using clustering, mapping, charting, and diagramming techniques, which she bases upon functions of the right and left sides of the brain. It is my experience in teaching writing that these techniques evoke strong responses: Some writers find them enormously helpful, and other writers respond quite negatively. I suggest you give them a serious try and see what happens. Shahrzad Moshiri was relatively new to my workshop when I offered Rico's suggestion for clustering as an exercise. She immediately found it productive, writing about her experience growing up in Shiraz, Iran:

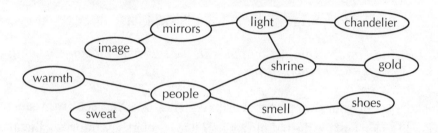

I took my shoes off and left them at the entrance to the shrine, at the top of the stairs with all the other shoes, old and new, hoping they would be there when I came back.

Shah Cheragh, the King of Light shrine, was my sanctuary; I put on a chadore and I was invisible, anonymous for hours. As I climbed up the stairs, the air was filled with the smell of rosewater with which the pilgrims had rubbed their faces and hands, and the musty sharp smell of dirty socks and sweaty bodies.

Many chambers opened off the main room where the body of the Blessed, wrapped in green silk cloth, was buried. The room was made of tiny rectangular mirrors, reflecting the light of the crystal chandeliers, hanging high from the ceilings. Images appeared and vanished in the broken light and faces became distorted, inhuman.

The tomb of the Blessed was surrounded by a chamber made of golden bars. I was engulfed in other people's bodies as I made my way around the room. The bars were cool and had the comfort of old and desperate kisses sealed on them by unknown pilgrims; I felt dizzy and comforted by the tide of human bodies pushing against my frame.

Making Lists

Lists and charts help you to see, help you to get out of the habitual rut of an accustomed way of thinking about something. They can help you to remember more exactly, or to imagine new possibilities for your fictional situation.

Suggestions for Using Lists

1. A listing exercise that was popular in the self-help movements of the 1970s and early 1980s is this:

Make a list of your own personal achievements, one for each five years of your life. Don't go for the big, glossy ones like scholarships or prizes. List the ones that really mattered psychologically at the time. Learning to tie your shoelaces, for example. The girl who said yes to a date when you thought she would say no. Then prioritize the list by omitting the two least important, then the next two least important, and so on, until you discover what was the very most important achievement of your life.

The first time I did it, this exercise taught me something very upsetting but important about myself. As a girl, I suffered from severe acne on my face. All through my adolescent years I believed I was ugly. When I was 35 or so I did this exercise in a group. When I prioritized my list, I was shaken to discover that the most important psychological achievement of my life (seen through the lens of that particular day) was not the birth of one of my children or having my libretto sung in Carnegie Hall; it was allowing my husband to stand before me and tell me I was beautiful without putting my hands over my face to hide it. On another day, in another year, doing the same exercise would bring about a different list of achievements and a different revelation.

2. Make a list of images from the past and/or the present.

Decide where they will come from, as one image from each five years of your life, or one image of each member of your family, or one from each school you attended, or one from each house you lived in, or one from each room in a certain house. Take the first image that pops into your mind and write it down. When you have completed the list, write freely, anything that comes to you.

3. List information about a character or subject in your writing.

List all the items in your character's pants pocket or handbag. List all the activities entered in each character's datebook for the coming week, all of the items in their bathroom cabinets. You will learn surprising things about your characters! You can also list pros and cons of a certain subject or action. List possible directions to go with a piece of writing.

Memories

The richest and purest source of imagery for our writing lies in the things we remember. Hemingway said, "Maybe away from Paris I could write about Paris as in Paris I could write about Michigan." All that we remember lies available within us, the treasure at the center of our lives. Best of all are memories we have held for a long time. If I were to ask you what is the most important thing that happened to you yesterday, you would probably feel a vague uncertainty; enough time has not elapsed to allow you to sort out yesterday's events. But in our memories of childhood, for example, most of the work of the artist has already been done by the unconscious: the images are polished, perfected, everything that is irrelevant has been eliminated. Everything that remains is crucial to the meaning, even if the meaning is hidden to us. (See my own story about this matter in Chapter One under the heading "Fear of the Truth About Ourselves.")

In memories from the deep past, all that remains is pure metaphor for an emotional truth. The meaning is in the image, the picture, the thing. According to William Carlos Williams there must be "no ideas but in things." In remembered images, the "thing" *embodies* the idea, as it does in our dreams.

81

Imitating the Work of Writers You Love or Hate

Imitation is a controversial method for teaching oneself to write (see further discussion in Chapter Six, on form) but I do think it is an excellent way to understand something of how another writer works at her or his craft. As a writing exercise, imitating another writer's style is nothing more than trying to walk a little way in his or her footsteps. Take a paragraph by Grace Paley or a poem by Adrienne Rich and try to write exactly in that voice, in that form. Change the pronouns and the images, but keep the sentence length, the line breaks, the rhythm. Then do the same with very different writers. Imitate a paragraph by Julio Cortazar and a poem by Christopher Bursk.

Take the third chapter of Steinbeck's *The Grapes of Wrath*. Only two and a half pages long, the chapter is a metaphor for the whole book, but it simply describes a turtle crossing a road. Change the turtle to a snake, a beetle, a water buffalo, a creature from another planet. Change the climate, change the kind of road.

Consider the chapter entitled "Time Passes" in Virginia Woolf's *To the Lighthouse*, in which she accomplishes a huge shift in the book with a little chapter of pure description. Write a purely descriptive passage that means something other than just the objects described.

An example of imitation of style is an exercise in Peter Elbow's *Writing with Power*. He suggests following the example of Wallace Stevens's "13 Ways of Looking at a Blackbird" in which Stevens writes 13 short verses giving different images of blackbirds. After writing thirteen "tiny stanzas about [a] cherry tree," Elbow discovers, "I see now that it is about missing the house on Percival Street where we used to live....If I had tried to write a poem about missing that house, it probably would have been terrible. Being stuck with having to write tiny stanzas about the cherry tree did it for me."

WHAT ABOUT PRIVACY?

Well, yes. Privacy is a problem. Jane Yolen, who has published more than 130 children's and adult books, has this to say:

> The first warning or rule of journal keeping is this: anything you put down *may* be made public. And if, perchance, you become famous—or close to someone famous—it probably *will*. If you lock your journal away, some smart aleck will find the key. If you ask your heirs to burn your papers, they will first take a trip to the xerographers. And any code designed by mortal man or woman can be broken by a computer in record time. So...write down only what you would not be embarrassed to see in print.

She's right, of course. To the extent that I write openly in my journal, my life is an open book. Someone, someday, will read it, whether it is published or not. And there are some things—not many, but some—that I do not write in my journal. Everyone's boundaries are his or her own; what would be intolerable to one is of no consequence to another. I have more than one friend who writes journals in times of great stress and then destroys them. I know the danger in keeping a journal. Someone may know who I really am. Or more accurately, someone may know who I am in the moments of the day when I am writing, and mistakenly think I'm like that all the time. Because sadness drives me to my journal much more than celebration drives me there, someone reading my journal could conclude that I am sad much more of the time than is true.

I can't help that. My journal is crucial to me. If I were to live by the restriction that I would write down only what I would not be embarrassed to see in print, I think I would have to stop writing altogether.

In the short run, there are ways to protect yourself. Lock your journal up, or put it in a notebook in plain sight, but mark it "Notes from old courses" or "Genealogy" or anything of minimal interest to somebody else.

My own advice is, write. *Write.* Even if there is no way to protect yourself for eternity. Kafka was correct: "Writing means revealing oneself to excess." Take whatever comes. If someone doesn't like it, that's too bad. Your job is to write.

EXERCISE 5:

Write Your Feelings

Where there is strong emotion expressed honestly, with no holds barred, language can become white-hot, true, effective. Ken Macrorie, author of *Telling Writing*, relates an incident in which a young student insists he cannot write an angry monologue. Macrorie instructs him to go home, stand behind his father's chair as his father is reading the newspaper, pour a glass of cold water on his father's head, and listen to what he says. He reports that the student successfully wrote an angry monologue after following his advice.

A young woman once told me that she was completely blocked in her writing: "All I feel is angry, and I can't write." She had been in my workshop for some time, and I felt that her statement was related to her writing block. I asked her to write for 10 minutes—nothing but four-letter words.

She came back to me, her face shining, and showed me her pages. The four-letter word of choice began small and got bigger and bigger until on the last pages there was one word per page. In the next few days she wrote a poem which later was published in *Peregrine*.

Anger is not the only emotional wellspring of good writing. Our personal history is full of deeply emotional experiences: joy, sorrow, love, fear, shame...

When I led a workshop in Japan, a young woman named C. Misa Sugiura wrote the following poem in response to an exercise. Misa had gone to elementary school in America, and the poem comes from a deep emotional experience—the shame a child feels when ridiculed.

When I was little,
people laughed at me
and called me
flatface.
They pulled their eyes into
slits
and said,
"Me Chinese!"
and laughed.

I didn't know my
face was flat
so I went home
and looked in the mirror
to see,
but all I saw was my
face.
It wasn't flat,
was it?

And I wasn't Chinese,
but I looked in the mirror anyway
and my eyes looked like
eyes.
Didn't they?

So I went to school
and said, "I'm Japanese and
my face
is like yours,
isn't it?"
And they said,
"No.
It isn't!

It's flat like a pancake.
Me Japanese pancake-face!"
And they laughed.

And I went home again
and I looked in the mirror
and I cried because
they were right.

To write this kind of experience so honestly is to be, at least in part, healed of it. Misa's poem is brilliant work. She allows us to go all the way into the experience of a young girl; she does not try, even at the end, to "fix it" for us. The child internalizes the taunts of her tormenters, which is the tragedy. Allowing us to feel it is the art. Misa shows us; she does not analyze or interpret.

By going back into that time, the writer, too, can freshly see the suffering child and can begin to heal her. Misa wrote at the bottom of the page that held the poem: "Dear Pat, Thank you so much for speaking and helping me write this—and helping me *live!*" It is what we do for one another, when we help each other to write and receive that writing tenderly. We help one another to *live.* In the best of all possible writing worlds, a writer has a community of supportive friends who evoke and respond to each other's work in ways that strengthen the work and the writers themselves. For every writer, however, the journal can be a safe place to write all of the heart's secrets and begin to heal some of the heart's wounds. It can also be the hidden place where powerful writing—great art—is conceived and nurtured.

FINDING YOUR OWN VOICE AND USING OTHER VOICES

*I*f I were asked to name one thing that this entire book is about, I would say it is about finding your own voice and using it. I believe you cannot truly write in the voice of various characters until you have found your own.

FINDING YOUR VOICE

We each have at least one voice; some of us have several. My primary voice is Midwestern. It was born in Douglas County, Missouri, grew up in St. Louis, lived for a while on the West Coast, and settled down in Massachusetts. When I talk to my children, they tease me because there are a few words that still come out of my mouth in the shape of Ozark pronunciation. I no longer say a woman "warshes and rinches" the clothes (although I can do that perfectly if I want to write a character who lives in Mansfield, Missouri), but I still ask my granddaughter, Sarah, "Wouldja like a glass of myelk, sweetheart?" As they laugh at me, I have a flash of myself at a country farmhouse table, my own grandmother saying to me, "Wouldja like some goat's myelk, honey?" Something in me doesn't want to let that pronunciation go. It is my own first voice; it is my treasure; it is what I know by heart.

We have been trained to distrust our original voices. When I was in college in Nashville, Tennessee, a speech teacher stood before a class of Southern and Midwestern young people and said that we must get rid of our regional speech and learn to speak what he called General American. General speech—general writing—is as boring as any other generality.

Francis Scott Fitzgerald warned, "Start out with an individual and you have created a type—start out with a type and you have created nothing." In other words, the *particular* is universal. Advertising firms know this: If you want to communicate to me the fact that millions of people are starving in Africa, you do not print statistics. You show me one child holding an empty bowl, his skin gray and tight over his distended belly, flies crawling on the rims of his eyelids. I see one child, and I grasp famine. Similarly, if you allow your characters to speak in your own unique, quirky, individual voice, they will be speaking a language that is real, a language that can be deeply felt and understood by others.

It has been reported that Grace Paley tells her students in every writing course, "If you say what's on your mind in the language that comes to you from your parents and your street and friends, you'll probably say something beautiful."

My work among women in low-income housing projects has taught me about voice. Everyone has at least one strong, beautiful, perfectly learned voice. And if a person uses that voice with utter abandon and confidence, art happens.

The piece that follows was written by Diane Mercier, one of the writers in my workshop for women in housing projects. Diane was born in the projects, lived for a time in an orphanage, and dropped out of school when she was 15 years old. She was early pregnant, early left alone with three children. Her first words to me were spoken as she stood half in, half out of the doorway to the office where I was holding a free workshop for women in the shadow of the huge, abandoned mills along the river: "I can't write nothin'; I ain't gonna write nothin'."

Something in me causes my heart to leap with joy when someone throws down that sort of gauntlet. In my mind I cry out, "Oh, yes, you can! *Get in here!*" But of course I reassured her, "That's all right, you don't have to write. We're glad you're here. You can just listen if you want to."

Diane has one perfect voice for writing. No one can write that voice better, more brilliantly, more accurately than Diane. It is the voice of a woman caught—for now—in poverty in America at the end of the 20th century. It has traces of French-Canadian immigrants in it; it has western Massachusetts milltown dialect in it. Using that voice with confidence and abandon is Diane's art form. This piece was published anonymously in *In Our Own Voices,* a collection of writings by women in housing projects. But as a result of writing with other women in my workshop, Diane's confidence has grown; she has given me permission to include it here under her own name.

What Keeps Me Ticking

What keeps me ticking? My mom? I'm not sure. All my mind can think of, is how come you never say I love you, but you listen to my sister, but never to me? You always use bad language at me. I guess that's the only way you can say I love you. I ask you a simple question; you say get away.

I grow up quiet, shy, and stay to myself. People say come and visit. I don't bother. I had to learn about life on my own because you never wanted to talk about it: what would happen when I grew up, having a baby, having my own responsibility. Mom, I wish I could talk to you, but I'm afraid to even say a word to you. I can't even say I love you; only in my mind I can say, I love you. If only you knew, but something is holding me back. There is something, but I can't put it into words. There's a dark secret you're keeping from me, but I wish I knew. If only you knew that I have questions to ask you. But I don't dare, so I stay to myself.

My sister doesn't like me because I am me: a bitch. My brother doesn't like me, because I'm a bitch. They think I won't find them out, but other people talk. They hold it against me for going out with a black man, but it's me who has to live with him, not them.

Maybe that's why I stay with him, to get even with them. They feel sorry for my daughters because they're half and half, half French and half black Puerto Rican. They wish I would go out with my own kind. Keep wishing, people! I love him in some way. Everyone is the same inside and out. So what he treats me wrong? Sometimes he can be nice. Everyone has a different side to them.

My family thinks no one is better than them. If only they knew how I feel! Maybe they will never find out; I keep myself to me. I want to find out the dark side of me, what keeps me all closed up, what I want. I won't let people know me well, because I'm afraid people won't like me if they know the dark side. Maybe that's why it's taking long to find out what it is. I feel so sad, so I keep to myself, don't bother no one, so I can't get blamed for it. Life will go on. My daughters will grow up. Maybe I will be able to tell them; I hope so.

I can remember a lot, no one even has to tell me. I was this way, I can feel the way, I can picture myself there at school. I just stay to myself, people calling me names. If only they knew what made me this way. My mom would never talk to me. She talked to my sister. If I stayed in my room, she never even bothered me. Also she would send me to the store. Whoopie! I get to go out! I always stayed in, never liked to go outside, afraid of people calling me names: "You're nasty looking!" or "You're too fat!" so I wouldn't eat. In the Job Corps, I wouldn't eat because my mom wouldn't send me any money to come home.

Because my niece died at two, I almost sliced my wrists. Something told me not to. Something told me to keep on living, find out what you want, what you are about. My sister will never change. There's always the same fight for attention, my brother too. I just sit back and watch. I wish I could find out who I am, what I want in life.

Diane has lived in only one circumstance in her entire life: housing projects in western Massachusetts. At this time she has only one voice, but she has learned that voice perfectly, and she can use it. I would wish for her many other voices. I would wish for her a full knowledge of the work of Woolf, O'Connor, Paley, Olds—the writers I have most loved—and those I respect but do not know as well. But not at the cost of losing her own greatest treasure: her own primal voice.

I believe that many writers who write in academic forms are using only one voice: the voice of the academy. Hidden in every one of their brains is another voice: the voice of those whom writer Paule Marshall in an article in the *New York Times Book Review* called "the poets in the kitchen." We all have the voice of our mothers at the kitchen table, the voice of our fathers in the workplace, the voices of the kids on the playgrounds where we fought our early battles. Marshall is talking about her own people, immigrants from Barbados, but she could have been talking about my people in the Ozark mountains, or Diane's people in the housing projects of Chicopee.

> Using everyday speech, the simple commonplace words—but always with imagination and skill—they gave voice to the most complex ideas. Flannery O'Connor would have approved of how they made ordinary language work, as she put it, "double-time," stretching, shading, deepening its meaning. Like Joseph Conrad they were always trying to infuse new life in the "old old words worn thin...by...careless usage." And the goals of their oral art were the same as his: "to make you hear, to make you feel...to make you *see*."

Write in your own native voice. That is where you will teach yourself how to write. No one knows that language as perfectly as you know it. Before you try to write in other voices, recover the use of the native tongue that is yours and yours alone.

Another member of my Chicopee workshop, Enid Santiago Welch, leads a workshop for children in her neighborhood. It is astonishing what power and natural artistry these children possess! The poem that follows is written by 10-year-old Robert Hastings:

Weed

It is life.
It grows from the ground.
It is ground up like meat.
It gives him a sharp and good feeling,
that gives me a sharp and painful anger.
He rolls it like a red carpet
and licks it like a lollipop.
My anger gets deeper
as the smell gets worse.
As he smokes me I get hotter and hotter.
He smokes me like I'm green.

Do not mistake my meaning; I am not saying that Robert will not benefit from training in his art. Nor am I saying that the use of my mother's Ozark dialect is sufficient for the writing I want to do, nor that Diane's use of the language she has learned in the housing projects is sufficient to express the rage and hunger and beauty that is in her mind. It is not enough. No amount of learning is enough. I will always be learning, trying, reaching, studying, and I hope that Diane and Robert will, too. It is, however, crucial that we recognize the native genius, the natural artist, that is in us all. Our own first voice is the absolutely necessary starting point, and it will always be the point of our greatest authority.

EXERCISE 6:

Taking a Risk

In my experience, people most often discover their own true voices when they are writing out of deep personal feeling. Only then does the frightened writer care so much about the subject that he or she forgets to be afraid. Self-consciousness falls away, and voice becomes true and strong.

I agree with Carolee Schneemann, who wrote in *More Than Meat Joy*: "Our best developments grow from works which initially strike us as 'too much.'...We persevere with that strange joy and agitation by which we sense unpredictable rewards from our relationship to them." So, write something brave. Write something that feels too huge, or too dangerous, to tell.

Barbara Ganzel is one of the bravest writers I have had in a workshop. In her book *An Afterlife for Children,* she writes about the experience of being a patient in mental hospitals. In the following poem, she writes about the death of her husband:

Two People Dying

He made his last volitional move
with his mouth.
He puckered towards me,
and I kissed him.
Then all that was left were his eyes,
and it's not true,
it's a lie what they say
about reading the whole human,
his pain,
what he needs,
what hunger—
about reading what's most important
from someone else's eyes.

All I could do   (*how can I shout this?*)
was climb under the tubes and the lines, all
his external arteries, to the man in the middle.
I would hold him and
feel his heart through the front of my chest
and trade him heat, body heat.

Days and months, trading life through our skins,
while the pump clicked through its cycle for food, and
the condenser chugged thin air into thick air, and the
shifts changed.

EXERCISE 7:

Surprise Yourself

Often writers are blocked because they are stuck in one way of doing writing: one form, one style, or one (usually derived) voice that is not their own natural way of speaking. Surprise yourself: write something that is different from your usual writing. One way to jar yourself out of habitual patterns is to write a few sentences in which the second half of each sentence does not make sense with the first half. Everything comes from your own mind, and so there will be another, and perhaps surprising, kind of sense.

Dorothea Kissam writes:

During a weekend writing retreat, Pat asked us to take ten minutes to write disassociated words or phrases. In other words, to write off the top of our heads. I found this exercise scary but revealing. It was hard for me to let go of my habit of carefully selecting every word. On the other hand, I felt fresh and renewed after the exercise.

First, an example of a poem that I had written the evening before in response to an object:

Ode to a Geode

The geode in my hand tonight
Holds me in familiar thrall.
I, in another time,
Have seen its gems before.

94

I must have walked the rocky place,
And found this special stone,
That opened like a treasure trough
To show Aladdin's cave.

Did the ancient sorcerer
Who created such a hoard
Of sparkling gems, hide them all
To ward off the alien eye?

The geode in my hand tonight,
Has glints of rose and gold.
But I knew its magic long ago,
And surrendered to its spell.

The next morning in response to Pat's request that we write "off the top of our heads," I wrote:

The wood beyond is alive—
I am alive, the wood is black.
The children smile then break apart.
It is hard to see to be to bear
To know what is beyond the
Glee—but it is there and must be so.
The fields are whitened by the snow.

It lies beyond—it stretches wide
A phantom spirit—gray and gaunt
Too long a whisper—gone beyond
To live to be alive if then to
Hang from a tree—a sumac cob
The red, the rust, the pink, the dusk—
The children smiling into the sun—
A gray rock, the night—to lean, to hold.

I am grateful to Dorothea for giving me these poems. In my opinion, the second poem holds more mystery, and allows me as reader more room to imagine, to find my own meanings, to be surprised and moved and changed. I believe that is so because it is more deeply—and riskily— Dorothea's own voice.

Writing in one's own voice may be assisted by getting rid of predictable patterns, but the true task, as Dorothea herself said, is "scary." These are the three most important guidelines:

1. Trust your own voice. (See "A Writer Is Someone Who Writes," Chapter One, and the section above.)
2. Tell your own truth, deeply, completely. (See Chapter One, on fear.)
3. After writing, don't "fix it" to death. (See "How to Revise" in Chapter Six.)

Going after our deepest truths and jarring ourselves out of predictable patterns are necessary for most of us, but one cannot do it all the time. We can also work at accessing our own voices in gentle ways.

EXERCISE 8:

Second Nature

A gentle exercise for writing in your own voice is to simply begin with an image from the natural world. Use the weather if it interests you. Begin by describing a rock, or an insect, or the way light comes through branches, or a single leaf. The important thing here is: don't try to be profound. Just write what you see, as clearly and exactly as you can. Profound meanings are hidden in concrete images; they will find you. Meanings will reveal themselves if you are true to what your eye sees.

Many times in this book I have mentioned my friend and writing companion Margaret Robison. She suffered a stroke three years ago, which left her paralyzed on her left side, and writes now sitting at a small table by a window where she can see the river that runs through the town where she lives. Yesterday she gave me this new poem, which caused me to think that, after all, the deepest and truest "exercise" is telling the truth of what you see and what it means to you, in your own voice:

Leaf

Gold leaves have gathered along the river banks—
birch, ash, catalpa. River rimmed in gold
like pages of an old holy book. The river too is sacred,
its mouth full of fishes and stones,
broad face reflecting the tree-covered mountain,
trees glorious in their reds and golds.
And sky—blue as eternity, its tumbled clouds
changing as quickly as one breath to the next.
Wind moves on the river's still surface
even as I watch, shattering images to light.
So many flashes and dots, like a dance of light
in an impressionist's eyes. Yet
what catches my attention this clear autumn day
is the single yellow leaf tumbling and drifting
in the air before me, making its way down to the river,
a leaf that once had the river of its own life flowing
down its center, spreading to tributaries
like my blood spreads through my body.
Dry now, the leaf has become a map,
a message from another time, an icon
for calling back this morning, this autumn, this life
that always renews itself like sacred words
that never die even after the pages they are written on
burn to ash, even after the ash itself rises
to become one with the air, even after
there's nothing left at all except the ache in the heart
to guide us home.

USING OTHER VOICES

Gaining skill in using other voices is a matter of remembering those we have heard and practicing those we want to learn. All of the voices we have lived among are still available to us in deep memory.

I learned my greatest lesson about voice while writing a novel, *If That Mockingbird Don't Sing.* One of the primary characters is a man named Elan, who grew up in rural poverty in the Appalachian mountains near Pineville, Kentucky. He had left that country, moved to St. Louis, become educated, and taken a position as a professor at a university. In the course of the novel, Elan receives a letter from his sister in the mountains, telling him that his mother has died. He begins his journey home.

When I was young, I worked for two summers in a church orphanage at Frakes, Kentucky, 30 miles into the mountains from Pineville. I wrote the novel 20 years later, having never been back to Kentucky. I felt that it was impossible for me to remember the speech of the people in those rickety houses on the mountainsides—it had been too long a time. I wrote Elan's trip back to his birthplace, allowing him to remember many things about his childhood. As he neared the house in which he had grown up, I became very concerned about how I was going to handle the meeting with his sister. I could see the wooded hillside, the abandoned cars, wrecked washing machines, the unpainted house, its porch hanging off the front like an old man's lower lip that doesn't completely close anymore. And standing on the porch I could see Elan's sister, a baby on her hip, her cotton dress bleached from hanging on the line in the sun. She was looking at him. He was in the car, looking at her. I could see them both as if I were there. My only option was to have her be silent. I could not remember accurately enough to let her speak.

Feeling upset and agitated, I left my typewriter, went upstairs, and took a shower. (I do that when I am writing intensely. Nothing—*nothing*—washes away tangles in my mind like water pouring over my naked body.) Standing in the shower, water streaming over my head, I heard Elan's sister begin to speak in my mind with absolute clarity. I dashed out of the shower, ran downstairs to my typewriter, and banged out her speech dressed only "in my utter altogether."

It was one of the most ecstatic writing experiences I have ever had. Only later did I remember that I owned a small book by Glenn Evans, the longtime director of the orphanage where I worked. It was a collection of stories told by mountain people, in the dialect of that place. I searched for it and found it. I had not read it for 20 years. The dialect was exactly as I had written it.

In the novel, Elan's sister stands still on the porch, watches him get out of his car and walk toward her. Looking down at him from the porch, she says:

> Hit ain't quite the way I told it in the letter, Little Junior. Ma she didn't jist get sickly an then die. She did get sickly, years an years ago, but her dyin come from Papa took a shotgun to her head an blew her brains out all over theseyere walls an floor an bedcloths an ever'thang...

She tells him what her life has been like, what has happened since the murder, and why he must leave quickly. She tells him that she has married a man much older than herself, someone who will care for her and her child:

> —Love? Love ain't about no teenagers hangin out in the bushes. Love is pickin up the pieces of your Ma's brain, washin up the blood after birthin' your own Papa's child. Love is honorin. It's hangin on. Love ain't kissin in the back seat at the picture show. It's need, that's what it is. Need.

When the reader turns the page, Elan is in Pineville, parked outside the jailhouse. He is thinking, in the language he has learned beyond the mountains, whether or not he will go into the jail to see his father.

When we are using voices that are not deeply embedded in our own memory, we have to do research and practice. When I was writing my one-woman play, *Berries Red,* I wanted to include a monologue by a black woman based on a story a friend, Ruby James, had told me about how she stood on the back porch in winter as a young girl, washing clothes. She described her own suffering and ended the story with: "My mama didn't have no right to do that to me, even if her mama *was* a slave." I wrote the monologue, but I did not trust my memory of the dialect, and so I called a composer with whom I have collaborated on gospel music, Flo Clark, and asked her to check it for me. There were four or five words that she suggested I change. Anytime we are using a dialect we do not know by heart, it is crucial to check it with someone who can catch the subtle errors.

The primary reason we are told in all writing books to write about what we know best is this: what we know best will most likely be written in an accurate voice. The greatest enemy of accurate voice is not ignorance, however, but tension. Try to relax, try to let yourself play. Voices are outrageous; they do unexpected things.

EXERCISE 9:

Eavesdropping

This exercise can be fun and of enormous value to any writer who wants to use dialogue. (And who doesn't!)

Go to an informal public eating place—a coffee shop or fast-food restaurant. Order something to drink, open your journal, and eavesdrop. Write down fragments of what people say. Your purpose is not to catch the whole conversation (that could be immoral, if not illegal!) but to capture the way people really talk. People talk in fragmentary sentences, in slang, in cliché, and in code. Enormous information about a person is revealed in his or her speech: nationality, class, culture, gender, education, taste, preferences. The woman on the train who giggles to her friend, "Yeah, honey, and she got warts in her *'gina!'*" communicates to me, sitting in the seat across the aisle, much more about herself than she might guess.

Tanyss Rhea Martula is a playwright who participates in my workshops

100

and has led playwriting workshops for Amherst Writers & Artists. About the example that follows, Tanyss writes:

I always keep a little notebook in my purse for writing down "catchy" phrases that I hear on just ordinary days. I jotted down some of these lines in that notebook after overhearing (eavesdropping really, I was so fascinated by something that sounded like a whole language unto itself) a couple of construction workers talking at a table next to me at Burger King. I have indicated for a theatrical scene that the roles could be played by men or women.

Burger King

(*Two construction workers are seated at a table in Burger King. They are talking. One worker's back is almost completely to the audience. While eating a Whopper and french fries, he/she responds only with nods or inaudible mumbling throughout the conversation. The other worker, who is drinking a cup of coffee, sits across the table at a slight diagonal to the first worker so that his/her face is visible to the audience as she/he speaks.*)

Who gives a shit? I'm not gonna rip all that shit out. Shit. I mean that's his goddamned shit. Why should I shit that?

I did a job like that over at my mother's. Never been through so much shit. With the floor. With my mother. Shit. Rippin' the old shit up. Then, puttin' in all the new shit, which won't last shit. Then, the goddamned doors and all that shit. Only took one goddamned weekend, but, hell, it was shit. Didn't get out on the golf course or nothin'. Just shittin' around inside.

Yeah, ya gotta rip the shit out of it. Then, put down the plywood, as long as there's no shit under the sub-flooring. Then, you put the shit on top of that. That's another thing, wanta finish this kind of shit-work before spring. Bein' inside all the time is shit. Makes me wanta shit in my pants. Shit, that's why I don't moonlight or nothin'. I don't give a shit, the extra bucks ain't worth the shit ya gotta put up with.

Now he comes out with 15 hours more on the work order. I don't take that kinda shit. Next he's gonna tell me I'm doin' a shitty job. What a shithead.

(Pause)

Shit, let's get the fuck out of here. Don't know how you can eat that shit anyway.

(The two workers exit.)

Write from Different Points of View

An excellent way to study the difference between voices is to write a report of the same incident from the point of view of two characters who feel very differently about a subject. For instance, a teenager and her mother, after the mother has opened a letter addressed to the girl. Or a child after a water pistol fight in a grandmother's living room, as in the following example:

From the point of view of the six-year-old with the water pistol: "Cool, man! I got 'im, Gramma! I got 'im right between the eyes! Man! Did you see that? Zap! Pow!"

From the point of view of the grandmother: "Eric, you have disobeyed me; you have used that gun with water in it, and I told you absolutely you could not! You have spilled water on my Persian rug! Furthermore, young man, you have hurt his eye..."

No matter how skilled you become in using voices other than your own, do not lose or underestimate that first voice, the voice you learned at home. Allow it to come up from deep inside yourself. Allow it to take over and talk through you onto your page.

Accepting and using your own voice will help you to truly hear and be able to use other voices.

THE FORM
YOUR WRITING TAKES

There is abroad in the land a belief that a writer must be identified by one genre, one single portion of the writing life, much as a side of beef is cut into greater and lesser degrees of prime. In my opinion, the pressure on writers toward specialization is disastrous to literature.

THE VALUE OF NOT BEING LIMITED
TO ONE GENRE

When I planted an apple tree in my yard, I learned that I wouldn't have apples unless I planted two trees, *of different kinds!* Literature, like trees, needs cross-fertilization. If variety is essential to apples, it is at least desirable in the written arts. Theater needs poetry, the novel needs masterful dialogue, songwriters need to be able to follow a narrative line. I do not love genre-specific workshops. I love the rich and fertile give-and-take when writers are working in varying forms. A fiction writer learns how to write dialogue by listening to two workshop members read aloud the scene a third workshop member, a playwright, has brought to the meeting. A poet learns specific, concrete use of imagery by listening to a brilliant prose description of a bullfrog in a pond at the edge of a country road in spring.

Furthermore, a writer needs the refreshment of various forms. In the workshops I lead, we write two, sometimes three times in one evening session. Once in a while someone writes three separate, wonderful poems in one evening. Some writers can write three sections of a novel-in-progress. But most mortals, like myself, may write one prose piece, one journal entry, and—if we are especially "hot"—one poem.

At issue here is the concept I have discussed earlier: Shawn's statement that "form is the shape of content." Flannery O'Connor put it similarly: "The more you write, the more you will realize that the form is organic, that it is something that grows out of the material, that the form of each story is unique." Except in very rigid forms where content must be fitted to a form, such as the mystery novel, where clue must pile upon clue and everything lead to a conclusion that is known by the writer at or near the beginning; or in the "formula" fiction of romance novels; or in classic forms such as the sonnet in poetry, the traditional Broadway musical, and so forth, *form is the shape of content* and will emerge by itself when the writer is fully engaged in the content.

Because the intention of this book is to free the writer from all that would restrict or hamper the imagination, there is a danger of underestimating the importance of form. There is a paradox here: Form is the shape of content, and yet all written content has a form.

In my experience, poetry holds the most confusion and difficulty for beginning writers. Many, many times writers have said to me, "I would love to write a poem sometimes, but I have no idea what a poem *is,* or how to go about it."

Everyone has the music of language, and everyone can write poems. What is wrong with most beginning poetry is its painful effort to *sound like a poem.* What is most needed is trust in the music of the language as we use it naturally.

But writing a poem is putting that naturally used language into a form. In this chapter I spend considerable time on form in the poem for these two reasons: Poetry belongs to everyone, and in spite of or in addition to everything I say about allowing form to emerge from content, understanding some basic things about form can enlarge the possibilities open to a writer.

How Do You Write a Poem?

This is a good time to be a poet, because our freedom is great. We have models, pioneers, practitioners who have opened difficult breaches in the walls of tradition and taboo and have broken down much of the tyranny of fashion. For women writing today this is especially true; when I was a college student in the 1950s there was literally no mention of women writers beyond a token poem by Emily Dickinson, and that one of her least challenging. In Ireland, in 1993, Emily Dickinson is still the only woman among 40 poets in the text for Leaving Certificate which marks the end of high school. When I was a young student, I knew the names of Marianne Moore and Virginia Woolf but was never required to read their work. There was no mention of Sylvia Plath or Anne Sexton, who were for the first time naming the condition, describing the geography, of women of my generation. I was middle-aged and they were long dead by their own hands before I knew what they had done for me.

Margaret Robison tells this story: When she was serving as Poet in the Schools in Holyoke, Massachusetts, there was a little boy who wrote prose but could not write a poem. When Margaret took the children to a nursing home, this little boy became friends with a 98-year-old woman named Emma. One day Emma gave him an orange. Later, Margaret asked the children to write about their experiences in the nursing home, and the time came for the little boy to read what he had written. "Nothing," Margaret says. "Flat. Then he came to the part about the orange, and the words sang—you could just taste that orange!" She made no comment to him about it, but asked him to read what he had written again, out loud, to her. He read it. She asked him to read it again. Still nothing. She had him read it three times, and after the third time, he put his hand over his heart and shouted, "It's poetry! I can hear it in my heart when it's poetry!"

106

What makes a poem a poem? There was a time when we could have said easily, "Why, a regular meter (preferably iambic pentameter) and end rhymed lines." No longer. I think only two things can be said of every poem: (1) it gives the reader a complete experience, and (2) it is language intensified. In addition to those, it may rhyme, it may not. It may be in a traditional stanza pattern, it may not. We even have "prose poems" now.

A poem invites something to happen in the reader. It is a country in which the reader may have an experience of his or her own, other than simply observing the emotion of the poet. If the poem is simply "Oh, how I suffered when Grandpa died," we may pity the poet, but we do not suffer grief. If the poem, however, shows us an old man walking toward a child, shows us the child in a detail as clear as her toes in her sandals, and lets us see something happen through the eyes of the child—as in this poem by Enid Santiago Welch, of my Chicopee workshop—we may feel within ourselves some response.

Abuelo

His shirt was blue.
I remember my mama said,
"Enid, tu abuelo,"
your grandfather.

The dirt road surrounded him.
There were mounds of piled earth
on both sides of the dirt road.
He was walking toward us.
My mama let go of my hand.

I had never seen my *abuelo*.
My toes curled down
into my sandals.

The truck came.
Abuelo's shirt

was underneath the truck's tire;
it was red now.
The cement truck with its dotted back
turned and turned in place.

My mother covered my eyes.

I like to think a good poet (any good writer, in fact) is like a set designer in theater; the poet creates the scene in which the reader is the actor. The reader may inhabit the body of the narrator, as in Enid's poem, or of the protagonist, as in Teresa Pfeifer's poem illustrating Exercise 25 (see Chapter Nine), in which we experience the poem as the "you" who breaks bread "into the center of your large green net." In either case, the reader has his or her own experience, observing the violent death of *Abuelo* in Enid's poem, or defending and releasing the helpless fish in Teresa's.

How do you make that possible? How do you intensify language and invite the reader into an experience that may not even be your own experience?

How *do* you write a poem?
1. Try.
2. Above all, trust concrete images.
3. Avoid "literary" language; use language that is natural to you.
4. Revise. Ask yourself if you have reached the deepest truth that is in you, seen it as clearly as it is in you to see, and given that clarity and truth to the reader. Go back over your poem and see what you can omit without losing anything essential. Try different line formations; breaking a line in the middle of a phrase can sometimes enhance the meaning of both lines. Let every line have some significance, some weight of its own. (Revising is covered in more detail later in this chapter.)
5. Have a sense of "play." Experiment with disconnections. Surprise yourself.
6. Let the shape of the poem on the page be satisfying.

7. Trust your reader. Avoid preaching; don't tell your reader what she or he can be trusted to discover. Margaret Robison says that the end of a poem should always open out to wider significance. Often the best way to end a poem is with a concrete image. In Enid's poem above, the image of the mother covering the child's eyes tells us everything we need to know about the event, the mother, the child. It opens out to the significance of the event, gives us room to imagine, to linger in the experience of being the child, being the adult woman remembering, being the mother trying to protect the child, being the grandfather, being the truck driver. It does not "close down" as it would if the last line were something like "Oh, it hurt me so much," or "my mother tried to protect me." Instead of telling us, the poet allows us to see. I have been there; at the end of the poem I have my own feelings and meanings to sort out. In that sense, every good poem is a collaboration between the writer and the reader.

On Unrhymed Poetry

The dominant form of poetry in America at this time does not use end rhyme, and even occasional internal rhyme is not common. Like many beginning poets, I started writing with end rhyme and internal rhyme. I felt uneasy and uncomfortable with what at that time was called free verse.

When I began to try to write without rhyme, it seemed my images were naked, and I felt exposed, alone with my images and what they might mean if I should reveal them to myself and to others. It was frightening because the music of rhyme had served as a kind of safety net under the tightrope a poet has to walk. It gave the safety of structure even if all else failed.

For a long time I abandoned rhyme entirely, feeling that it was absolutely necessary to allow a poem to grow as the form my voice took, rather than to try to make my voice fit a form. Now, having written without rhyme for years, I am coming back to it, loving it, using it again. But now I understand that there are times when rhyme serves the spirit and there are times when it gets in the way. I had to be a fairly mature writer before I could tell which was which in my own writing life.

The example below, by Ann Stokes, is a poem that has been crafted with great care and without the use of rhyme. Gothics is one of the Adirondack mountains.

Gothics

The wild gusts of heaven have
thrilled this mountain. The winds
have swept so long, rounded the
rock cleaned the rock, undone
the evergreen roots down to the moss
we lay our heads upon
seven thousand years later.

Once clothed it now bares scars,
muted colors of the stone
that is its bone and surface.
Stretching, stretching under every
heat of those quicksun seasons.

Its heart cannot contain itself.
Awaits the rush of blue
the first and last pink
sudden out and downpourings
a peregrine whose wingtips
hold its name.

Close to those wings the mountain
surrenders to aging, so customary
by now; invisible, in slides, gashes
stark in the light the moon
throws without cover.
Its ridge rises to collide with
the setting moon in ancient reassurance.

Everything comes down upon it,
is thundered at it. Even the
mist does not hover but enters
to give moist rest. Gothics takes
all and gives back all
in astounded silence.

On Rhyme

Rhyme is magic. In English, rhyme is a tool of the poet, the songwriter, and even the prose writer, playwright, and nonfiction writer. In some literary periods in the English language, end rhyme in a regular pattern has been so important as to be required of any piece of writing with the temerity to call itself a poem.

Most of us grew up listening to rhymed language, whether it was *Jack Sprat could eat no fat,* the hymns we heard in church, certain commercials like the very first singing commercial on radio, which I remember as *I'm Chiquita banana, and I'm here to say, bananas must be treated in a special way...,* or on the playground: *Step on a crack, Break your mother's back.* Rhyme is, in short, our mother tongue.

But in a recent issue picked at random from my pile, the *American Poetry Review* had published 63 poems by 31 poets, and not a single one rhymed. There were two poems that had occasional end rhyme, but in neither case was rhyme sufficient to appear more than accidental.

Writing, like the clothing we wear, has its fashions. There is some indication that rhyme has been out of fashion almost long enough to make it fashionable again: I recently saw an advertisement for an anthology of contemporary rhymed poetry.

It is an easy thing to say "Well, the hell with fashion!" To wear clothing that is out of fashion is sometimes desirable, but usually it is done intention-ally, to signify rebellion, farce, and so forth. So, too, in writing. If with serious intention you write a rhymed poem and use archaic words *(o'er, dasn't, 'twere,)* or worn-out rhymes (moon/june/croon/spoon), you will be repeat-ing patterns that others before you have made threadbare. On the other hand, if you use rhyme as Robert Frost and Audre Lorde did, true to the idiom of your own time, and if you accomplish that miraculous balance in which the rhymed poem, read aloud, seems to be effortless, natural speech, if the subject *matters,* and you have condensed language and heightened imagery and told the truth, then you have probably written an excellent con-temporary rhymed poem.

Read Robert Frost's poem "Stopping by Woods on a Snowy Evening" aloud to yourself, and notice how absolutely natural the language is. It is as if Frost were simply speaking, and speaking intimately to you. There is no strain, no hint of a word chosen for the sake of the rhyme. It seems absolutely effortless.

Look at the rhyme scheme: Every third line is the origin of the rhyme of the next stanza. That pattern, done so perfectly, so smoothly that it is almost invisible, almost inaudible, is what gives the poem its music. When the last line is repeated, word for word, we feel an almost ecstatic beauty, like a great "amen," perhaps without realizing that what gave that repeated line its power was the completion of a pattern started in line three of stanza one. The poem seduces us, tricks us, conceals an incredibly skilled craftsman at work—so skilled that his craft is invisible in the naturalness of ordinary speech.

Working to achieve a perfectly natural line of dialogue in a story or a play is different from working to achieve a rhymed stanza. In rhymed poetry we are assigning ourselves a musical as well as a conceptual task. And the ear is an exacting taskmaster.

Many writing teachers encourage their students to practice by working in traditional forms. I believe that learning traditional form is to writing poetry as learning to spell words correctly is to writing in general. Knowing the mechanics will not make you a writer. Nevertheless, knowing how to spell the words you say is a very helpful skill, and knowing the literary tradition from which you have come is helpful knowledge because it can increase your awareness of what is possible. It may sharpen your use of the language. Imitation, however, may block, inhibit, or intimidate your own originality. Examine yourself before you undertake this kind of exercise, and if you do undertake it, remember that it is not quite the same thing as the search for expression of your own vision in whatever form that vision takes.

Using a structured form does not cause me to say anything I do not want to say. It may cause me to say some things that I would not have said if I had not been searching for a way to complete a pattern; that is sometimes good, surprising, helpful. Quite often the necessity of my own meaning may cause me to abandon the pattern that I am trying to use. When an established form works well, it simply forces me to hone the cutting edge of my meaning through a discipline of the requirements of form in addition to the requirements of spirit.

Having abandoned rhyme in my own work for many years, I began to return to it by experimenting with the forms of nursery rhyme and schoolyard chant, believing after all that they were a kind of primal music in my memory. I was excited by my own discovery that there was a musical and rhythmic relationship between the song of revolution "We Shall Overcome" and the schoolyard chant "Mary has a boyfriend." It was as if there were a deep underground current of music from which we all have drunk, and for which we all thirst.

In a time of personal chaos I instinctively reached for the order of rhyme. The poem that follows was written as my clergyman husband and I were deciding to leave the church. I attempted to rhyme both ends of the lines with an a-b-a-b pattern without compromising the natural speech, but after 36 drafts, I allowed the left side to rhyme within the first or second word with *a b c b*, and the right with *a b a b*.

Letting Go

As a beggar, resting in the sun,
Peels off layers of her outer rags,
Astonished to discover that each one

Reveals another under it, her paper bags

Filling with the garments she had worn
When everything was harder, darker, colder;
As she feels the chill of being born
Again, wiser now, and older,

So I. Having shed the church in the belief
That one particular chill of letting go
Might be a kind of ultimate relief,
(A flat sun of contradiction, saying "No"

To winter, to the ice around the heart,)
Under vestments I am finding near the skin
Ragged garments where all distinctions start.
I blunder toward the person I had been

Before costuming for the beggar's part
And trying out in someone else's show.
Living now is nakedness of heart;
Dying—just another letting go.

The Importance of Reading Contemporary Poets

Two things are necessary, and they are somewhat paradoxical: you must protect your voice, your unique vision, and you must be aware of—indeed companioned by—other writers of your own generation. In everything that is important there also lies danger. The danger here should be stated first: You can lose your own focus, your own voice. When you are deeply involved in writing about your mother, it may not be a good idea to read other people's poems about their mothers.

That said, I suggest that you first get a good anthology of contemporary poetry, read until you find something in a poem you like, then stay there a while. You don't have to like it all. Try to listen to the unfamiliar voices, but allow yourself to be taught by those whose work you love and trust. Find someone in the anthology whose work moves you, and then buy that poet's collected work and study it.

Read aloud, read repeatedly. Read first as one person being spoken to by another person. Receive what is being given, spirit to spirit. Sometimes that takes a lot of readings. Read as a writer. Think about what the poet is doing and why. Think about the poem in writerly ways. How does the poet begin the poem? What is he or she doing with line breaks? How does it end and why? What discovery does the poet allow the reader to make for him or herself?

Read favorite poems onto an audiotape and listen as you drive. Memorize. Joseph Langland, who is known for his repertoire of memorized poetry, was once challenged by his friends, as they were swimming in the Mediterranean Sea, to quote poetry for 30 minutes while treading water. He met the challenge, and then set himself the task of driving from Amherst to Boston, a two-hour drive each way, quoting poems he knew by heart all the way to Boston and back without repeating a single poem. He did it. What a rich inner treasure Joe carries with him everywhere!

The person who reads widely and well will find his or her voice deepened and strengthened. Even so, there are times when the writer needs to put aside all other voices save his or her own.

Coming to believe that I had a voice of my own, that I could write poems, was the hardest thing I have ever done as a writer. Notice I did not say writing a poem was the hardest thing. Writing a poem is a little like walking on a narrow ledge—remember, when we were kids? It was so much easier if another person was there within reach—not that we touched that person, but just in case. I think you need friends when you are taking the risk of writing poems. Someone who will be gentle with you, rejoice when you achieve perfect balance, and help you a little when you lean too far to one side or the other.

Form from Content

The most important exercise I know to begin to write a poem is to ask, What matters? A poem must be about something that matters. The answer often comes in the form of a picture. Take it; that is your poem. No matter how inconsequential the picture may seem, write it down. Your mind has given you that picture as something that matters; writing, you will discover why.

Write until you have said what you want to say, and then break it into poem lines, seeing if there are words or phrases you can omit to make it cleaner, clearer, tighter.

In Margaret Robison's beautiful book-length poem *Red Creek: A Requiem*, there is the following excerpt, which taught me how to find poems of my own by asking, "What matters? What matters to me at this moment?"

> What matters, then?
> Poetry matters, and the line
> that will not break
> under the weight of history.
> What matters then?
> A single gardenia broken
> from the dark-leafed bush.
> What matters then?
> The dark-leafed bush.
> What matters then?
> The gardenia.

The Random-Word Poem

A writer in my workshop introduced me to an exercise she credited to poet Carolyn Forché. Like good folk songs, which change as they are passed from person to person, so this has no doubt altered in translation. This exercise springs me out of my habitual patterns, makes me think and write in fresh ways.

Make a list of 10 or 20 random nouns on one side of your paper, and a list of random modifiers on the opposite side. Then draw lines to make the most unlikely combinations of nouns and modifiers. Write a poem in which you use at least five of those unlikely phrases.

The following example is by Elizabeth Earl Phillips, a member of Peggy Gillespie's workshop in Amherst Writers & Artists:

Nouns	Modifiers
wallpaper	disjointed
hand saw	menacing
poplar	beached
sumac	scummy
Idaho	feathered
lunch box	scarred
line	cacophonous
plastic	steely
barnacle	mouldy
goalie	astigmatically
biscuit	ulcerated
truck	dusty
finger	smeared
	weathered
	claustrophobic

Windswept

A scarred black lunch box lay
      within a clump of ulcerated sumac
cautiously Ray and I
      pried its barnacled hinges open
inside was one steely biscuit

and a feathered hand saw
"Claustrophobic Idaho" was scratched
across the tin nameplate
a solemn whistle keened six
dusty trucks from the reservation
idled at the bleached mine gate
smeary children
too tired to cry
sucked weathered thumbs.

EXERCISE 13:

The Scrambled Poem

This is another playful exercise that helps to disconnect habitual ways of thinking. Write a simple little incident, a short narrative, beginning on line one, but using every fourth line on your page, skipping lines two and three. When you get to the bottom of the page, go back to the top and write on each second line. When you get to the bottom, go back to the top again and write on each third line. The scrambled result can be the raw material of a poem. Feel free to change, delete, or add to make your final poem, as Barbara Bosma Van Noord did in the work below, which won third prize in a contest sponsored by the literary journal *Oxalis:*

Light Shimmers into Nothingness

this June evening
just before the sun bows
all the way to the ground

light shimmers
into nothingness
down the length of the river.

no one has been this way
in a long time. the grass
springs back underfoot,

clumps of violets sprout
in the middle of the path,
sounds of water obligato nearby.

the small skull
that almost might have been
a dog's, faced the river
there, just off
the logging trail,
a skull too small for a deer

but with long leg bones.
there is still so much
unnamed, unknown,

so much the moss and mushroom
have reclaimed.
the continuous phonics

of the river,
there is that.
and its thick wintering over,

the road still
cut through the shallows.
the delicate haunch.

EXERCISE 14:

The Classic Poem

Using Millar Williams's book *Patterns of Poetry: An Encyclopedia of Forms*,
or any other good source of poetry forms, choose a classic form—sonnet,

haiku, sestina—and write a poem within that form. Or take as your model a familiar old song:

> Frankie and Johnny were sweethearts
> And oh, Lordy how they could love!
> They were true to each other,
> As true as the stars above—
> He was her man, but he done her wrong!

Write something in the form you have chosen, noticing matters of craft. For example, in "Frankie and Johnny," you might note the internal near rhyme (the repetition of "o" sounds in line two, and "oo" sounds in line three), the exact end rhyme on lines two and four, with the near rhyme in the "oth" of line three, and so forth. You may learn about using rhyme, near rhyme, particular stanza forms and such matters, by this kind of literal following of existing forms.

EXERCISE 15:

The Created Form

Make up your own (difficult, exacting, challenging) form and write a poem in that form, being as hard on yourself as possible, allowing yourself no easy solutions to difficult tasks.

The following poem, by Kate Gleason of my Amherst workshop, uses an unusual and provocative form: the break in the lines of the poem echoing visually the break that is being expressed in the words:

Fracture

Her father would break her	Bones
arm, almost kill her, would	have
jeer, on the one hand, at the idea	the consistency
that she still loved him, the other side	of igneous rock,
afraid, knowing she was	the one

most like the boy his father had
made him into, unable to say
stop, I don't care what
you do, you can't make me not
love you. Some fathers—
even the good times are
shaky. The heart is willing
but the body is too
weak. It's learned what it learned
in the dark
and passes it on like Northern Lights
ice acting as
a mirror to the fire storms
on the sun, flare-ups in
the light the color of a
hidden pilot, so blue it's
a flame, tear-shaped, blazing

shaped by fire.
When
fractures
heal
they leave
a space
that won't
close,
a way
to tell
weather,
a barometer
inside
the bone
now,
an ache
for storms.

How Do You Write Fiction?

I once watched a television interview in which Eudora Welty was asked whether her fiction was autobiographical or imagined. Her answer was something like this: "If I tell you it is autobiography, you will be embarrassed. If I tell you it is imagined, you will feel cheated. So I will tell you the truth: It is a mixture of both."

Ironically, all fiction is autobiography, and all autobiography is fiction. Even that which I may think is factual historical material is an interpretation, a version of the truth recorded from my own particular angle of vision.

What matters in fiction is what matters in poetry or plays or libretti or any art: the integrity, the honesty, the originality of the work. Integrity: what really matters. Honesty: courage. And how do you achieve originality? By being true to the unique angle of vision that is your own. In a classic book,

The Forms of Fiction, John Gardner and Lennis Dunlap list as "the most obvious" elements "shared by all good fiction, whatever form that fiction may take": *intellectual honesty, emotional honesty, and aesthetic validity.* This holds whether the source of the work is autobiographical or imagined.

Jane, a young writer in one of my workshops, did not want to write anything related to her own life. She wanted to write "fiction." In the first writing exercise, I suggested an image of someone holding a cup. Jane wrote a piece that on the surface seemed to be a clear and simple description of an action. A man and a woman were at a dining table. The woman had wrapped a teacup and saucer to give as a gift. The man wanted to see it; he opened the box, unwrapped the cup, dropped it, and broke it. There was not one word of overt "telling" about emotion; the writing was clean and strong and visually very satisfying. It was a brilliant piece of writing because at the end of the two or three handwritten pages everyone in the room knew that what had broken was the relationship. The writer knew it, too; she was trembling and very upset. I suspect her writing had shown her something that she did not fully consciously know. Certainly she had learned that it is a dangerous thing to write "fiction." Good fiction tells the truth.

At a workshop I led at the Graduate Theological Union in Berkeley, there was a retired minister among the students and lay people. The first time I had the group write, I put out on a cloth 30 or 40 random objects. Louis, the minister, chose the crystal ball. He wrote a rather stiff (frightened) small paragraph about the ball itself, describing a little chip in the smooth surface and giving a sermonic moral: All of us have chips in our perfection. It was writing as usual for him; part of his life work had been finding the meanings in ordinary things and lifting up those meanings for his people. I knew that I had to jar him loose from his habitual writing patterns if he was to write with integrity, honesty, and originality.

In the second writing exercise, I had everyone close her or his eyes, relax, and suggested, "Remember a time before this time, when you were younger than you are today, and find yourself standing in a doorway. What is the quality of light before you? What is the quality of light behind you? Is anyone near you, or are you all alone? Stay there as long as you want; if something begins to happen, let it happen. When you are ready, very quietly pick up your paper and write what happened, or what your eye sees, or anything else that comes to you to write."

Louis "found himself" standing in the doorway to his sister's bedroom, looking at her bed. Her violin was on the bed, the case open, the music stand holding the music for "Silent Night, Holy Night." When he read this to us, he began to cry and could not finish reading. We waited quietly for a bit, and then I asked him if it was okay for us to go on. He said he wanted us to know that his sister had committed suicide 35 years earlier, and he had never cried about it—not when she died, and not afterward. He apologized for crying.

I talked to Louis at length after the workshop session. I told him that I have cried many times when I read new material; I assured him that someone else would have that experience before the week of workshop was done, because when we write, we touch on our feelings, on our own personal stories, and emotion comes up inevitably. He said he knew that it was important, but he didn't want to write about his sister again. He was not a man who could cry; this was too dangerous. I supported him, I said I understood, and encouraged him to respect his own timing, his own way of processing things.

I had planned to use as an exercise the next day a poem by Sharon Olds called "The Takers," about one sister who pees on another. Siblings are a terrific source of writing material! But because of Louis's decision to avoid his sister, I changed my plan and put out a large collection of buttons from my mother's button box, suggesting that people choose buttons, describe the dress of two characters, and let the characters talk to each other. Louis took one button, described his sister's dress, and wept when he tried to read.

This went on for the entire week. Every exercise I gave turned for Louis into the image of his sister's room, her absence, his grief, and finally—his anger. On the last day, I suggested that people write a letter to someone else, or to the writer inside themselves. Louis wrote, of course, a letter to his sister. This time we all cried.

In the course of the week, Louis taught himself how to write. He wrote honestly, courageously, and with originality. That workshop was six years ago. In the intervening years I have listened to perhaps a thousand prose pieces, poems, scenes from plays, portions of novels, nonfiction fragments. Yet as if it were yesterday I remember a room as still as death, an open violin case, an abandoned music stand and the music...*Silent night, holy night, all is calm, all is bright....*

We all know how to write fiction. It is just another way to tell the truth.

On Craft

What about "craft"? What about writerly skills like plotting, character development, point of view, transitions? For the writer of fiction, as for the poet, as for all artists, learning craft is a lifetime process.

I said early in this book that in making art, desire is the soul, practice is the body. In the art called writing, however, I think we do not give ourselves or others credit for how much practice we have already had. The young woman, Jane, and the retired minister, Louis, wrote with such power on the first day of their first writing workshop because they, like all of us, had *practiced* telling stories since they were less than two years old. It counts for something, that practice. Writing is not so far removed from speech as some would have us believe; focused speech, speech that is full of emotion or clear intention is often excellent writing, *written on the air.*

We cannot learn too much. We cannot know too much. Everything we learn in our lives or in our conscious study of the work of others can enrich and deepen our writing. The study of how a man sits on a stool in the local diner, how his shirt does not meet the top of his blue jeans, how the dark hair on his back curls like a young child's hair (or bristles like the hair on a wild boar), or the study of how an old woman's body shrinks in the bed until the shape of her skeleton is visible under the parchment skin—this sort of study can be of vital importance to the craft of writing. And formal study of even the most daunting of academic texts enlarges the world of the writer. I am glad I read *Ulysses*—783 pages of one day in the life of a Dublin man—but it was painful. Only recently I read Carolyn Heilbrun's brilliant comparison of James Joyce and Virginia Woolf in *Hamlet's Mother and Other Women*. I wish I had read Heilbrun years earlier, and I wish it was required reading in all college literature programs. As Heilbrun points out, the two writers were born in the same year and died in the same year, but their lives and their work differed so much that in them, the great river of English literature divided, and all of us who write today drink from one or both streams. Such knowledge as I have of Joyce, Woolf, Eliot, Moore, and the rest has enriched me; but no more so, I am convinced, than knowing in the muscles of my back and the formation of my bones what poverty is—what it is to be the child of an uneducated, divorced working-class woman in America.

Life itself will happen to you; observe it. Form the habit of recording your observations in your journal. Live your own life thoughtfully, empathetically. Talk and listen. From these practices will come the most important things you need to know in order to create good fiction.

There are courses in fiction writing in every city and independent workshops in many communities, and all libraries are rich in resources for studying the art of fiction writing. John Gardner's books on fiction writing, Flannery O'Connor's on the short story, and Ursula LeGuin's on fantasy writing have been particularly helpful to me, as has *Points of View,* an anthology of short stories arranged to illustrate 11 different narrative points of view, edited by James Moffett and Kenneth R. McElhen. Janet Burroway's *Writing Fiction: A Guide to Narrative Craft* and Peter Elbow's *Writing without Teachers* and *Writing with Power* are excellent. In addition, Dorothea Brand, Natalie Goldberg, Ken Macrorie, Anne Bernays and Pamela Painter, Ray Bradbury, Brenda Ueland, Robin Behn and Chase Twichell, and Annie Dillard have written books for writers that I frequently recommend to others. *Writing from the Heart: A Book for Women Who Want to Write,* by Lesléa Newman, has a wealth of fiction writing exercises that are equally valuable for both men and women. *Poets & Writers Magazine,* the newsletter of the Associated Writing Programs (AWP), and articles in the *New York Times Book Review* are excellent sources of help for working writers.

The First Draft

Begin with an Image

Novelist and short-story writer Valerie Martin, writing in the *New York Times Book Review,* quotes many writers on how their work began and then observes:

> All of these descriptions have one thing in common: they begin with an image, coming from within or without, strangely persistent in the writer's imagination....The desire at the start is not to say anything, not to make meanings, but to create for the unwary reader a sudden experience of reality.

Begin with an image. See in your mind's eye a toy box, then move in closer and see the small, yellow Tonka truck tumbled on its side. Look at it closely; notice where the light falls, where the shadows rest. Now let your peripheral vision catch some other detail. Write it down. "What you *see,* write it in a book," was the command given to the ancient writer of the book of Revelation. It could not be said better today.

This is what kills fiction: that you should manipulate it, that you should coerce it, that you should think you can make fiction as you would make a batch of biscuits—by following a recipe. Fiction that is original, fiction that is *art,* must come from an engagement between the conscious and the unconscious mind. *What you see, write it...* and like Jane's cup and saucer, and Louis's music stand in an abandoned room, what you see will make your fiction for you. The meanings will be visible in the objects. Remember the words of William Carlos Williams: *No ideas but in things!*

Write a Complete First Draft without Editing

A first draft of an entire piece of fiction is a battle almost won. Write a complete first draft without too much looking back. Write instinctively, intuitively, without passing judgment. You can always go from vision (dream,

126

inspiration, what you see) to craft, but you cannot always go from craft to vision. Vision without craft may be raw, but craft without vision is dead.

Trust the Disconnections and the Gaps

If you have written what your eye first saw (say, the toy box) and you are stopped, see again. See something else. Take a leap to another image. Don't require of yourself that you understand the connection. Trust your unconscious mind; there is a connection, and it will reveal itself if you continue to be true to what you see. Some of the most brilliant things that happen in fiction occur when the writer allows what seems to be a disconnected image to lead him or her away from the line that was being taken. Often in workshop a writer will say, "Oh, I didn't see that myself," when in discussion someone points out a subtle metaphor that captures the whole of the writer's intent.

Surprise Yourself

Good teachers of fiction say it everywhere: No surprise for the writer, no surprise for the reader!

You must be surprised. You must be taken captive by the story that hides within what you see. Many writers have written about the strange way in which characters take over, take control, refuse to do what the writer wants them to do. John Fowles, in his notes on writing *The French Lieutenant's Woman,* describes such an experience:

> I was stuck this morning to find a good answer from Sarah at the climax of a scene. Characters sometimes reject all the possibilities one offers. They say, in effect: I would never say or do a thing like that. But they don't say what they would say; and one has to proceed negatively, by a very tedious coaxing kind of trial and error. After an hour over this one wretched sentence, I realized that she had in fact been telling me what to do: silence from her was better than any line she might have said.

How to Revise

Revision is absolutely necessary. A piece of writing that comes out whole and perfect is a miracle. Miracles happen, but not often. Revision is the second half—at least—of the act of writing. But there is great danger in revising if you do not know what is strongest and best in your own work. You need the response of others in order to learn about your strengths. There are specific guidelines for giving and receiving response in Part Two of this book, "Writing with Others."

Mary, a well-known visual artist, joined my workshop to write for children. For several weeks in my workshop her writing was frozen. The language reminded me of my own earliest experiences of reading: "Dick runs. Jane runs. Dick and Jane run." When a person's writing is stiff and controlled, I think sometimes of a wall behind which an amazingly beautiful wild creature is imprisoned, terrified, looking for an opening to freedom.

On the fifth session of the workshop, Mary suddenly wrote something entirely different, a letter to a former workshop leader who had hurt and embarrassed her, and it was white-hot with anger. "*You*," it said, "are the wicked stepmother. *You* look in the mirror and ask, *Mirror mirror on the wall, who's the fairest of them all?* You smile and comb your long black hair, and we sit in the ashes."

The workshop was stunned. The writing went on, powerful, free, full of imagery, metaphor, passion. When she finished, we spontaneously broke into applause. Mary couldn't believe it. She tried to tell us that it wasn't writing at all, she was just "taking a break" from her real writing work.

I told her, and others told her, how wonderful the writing was. We asked her to bring it back, typed, the following week, so we could see it in manuscript form.

At the next meeting, at our request, she began to read once more: "You are the wicked queen. You look in the mirror. You smile. We sit in the ashes." All the life, the passion, the driving intensity, was gone. And it was gone for good, because she had thrown the original manuscript into her dumpster, and it had disappeared into the town dump. What she had done is very

128

common: She had revised her work away from her own voice to some pre-conceived idea in her mind about what good writing should sound like. She had revised it to death.

But we had all heard something wonderful. Mary's own voice had made its appearance, and it was powerful. Once you have found a place of power inside yourself, it is like finding a new room that you didn't know existed beyond the wall of your usual habitation. Once you have found the way, you can go there again. Furthermore, there are rooms beyond rooms waiting for you to discover. Mary had found the opening in the wall. She was free. From that moment she began to teach herself how to write, but it was a process of coming to know what she does well, what her own strengths are, what her unique voice is, not what her weaknesses were, what she was doing wrong.

I could not have guessed what Mary's writing voice would be like. I have had this experience over and over again. Only by listening to what people write, and naming to them what is strong; only by patience, by waiting and listening, can I hope to catch the exact, exquisite pitch of genius that hides in a hurt or frightened writer. Once Mary began to write with freedom, once her own voice made its appearance, I could help her on the page to enlarge her own capacity, to learn to trust her own gifts, to recognize those times when she lost her footing. Until then, all a teacher can do is encourage, evoke, invite, and wait.

Mary is a sophisticated, urbane writer. She is one of the funniest people I have ever been privileged to have in a workshop. After two years of making us laugh until we were in profound disarray, she began a new children's book. She had taught herself how to write, and now the language was exactly right, the rhythms free and full, the book wild and witty and wise. At this time it is on its way to a second editor after one major publisher of children's books has returned it to Mary, saying that it came very close to acceptance.

EXERCISE 16:

Fact into Fiction

Sometimes beginning writers find it hard to break out of "fact" into "fiction." I have found this to be an excellent way to move through that block. First, choose a name with which you would be comfortable if it were your name. Where you have used "I" in the writing, change it to that name. Where you have "me" and "my," change it to "she" and "hers," or "he" and "his." Then add one small imagined detail: a hammer on the kitchen counter that wasn't really there; a toothbrush still damp in the medicine cabinet that was not really there. Once you begin imagining, you quickly see that fiction is always a mixture of what we have experienced and what we have imagined.

EXERCISE 17:

Begin with an Image

This is the most effective "open sesame" into writing that I know. I use it all the time. Begin with something your inner eye sees, allow your reader to see it clearly, and don't worry about where it is going. It will go, if you relax and invite anything at all to come. In the two short-short stories that follow, both writers were surprised by what came. In the first example, Pat Sackrey of my Amherst workshop began with an oak tree:

In the Woods

In winter, the red oak tree stands like a stag in the forest. It grows from the base of a giant granite rock that sits squat and silent—a great, grinning frog.

In summer, the tree has a heavy crown. It moves in any breeze. The rock turns green with lichen. Its scars hold tiny pools of rain where dragonflies drink.

The old woman who visits them stands watching for a while, uncertain. She takes off her shoes and climbs on the rock. She feels its age. It cools her feet. She kneels down and pushes her palms against rotting leaves on the rock's surface. The leaves are spongy, damp, and smell like earth.

In the small spot of sun, she takes off her clothes. She puts her hands softly against the tree, feeling its rough, channeled trunk and patches of damp, cool moss. She leans her body against the tree, pressing a little, and lets the breathing of her stomach move her gently back and forth. Holding the tree trunk in her arms, she curves her leg around it. She looks up the furrows of bark, up the gray, dark trunk, mottled in the sun. The tree, gently rolling in the summer wind, looks down on her.

The woman pushes her wrinkled breasts into the tree, feeling her nipples curve into its dark crevices. Her fingers smooth and stroke the lush emerald moss, softly, slowly. She begins to move up and down against the tree. As she breathes, she moans. Her foot pushes against the cool surface of the rock, pushing her into the tree. Holding the tree, looking straight up into its crown, she feels her face grow hot, sweat runs from under her arms, down her hips, down her legs, under her feet. Bits of moss and bark cling to her belly and thighs. Leaves grow from her tangled hair and her fingers appear as twigs. She sways as the wind blows through her. She extends by tendrils through rocky crevices into ancient depths of fallen leaves. Dragonflies drink her tears.

In the next example, Moya Hegerty, a nun who is a member of the workshop I lead annually in an Ursuline convent in Ireland, begins with a very concrete image:

Cow Dung

Plonk! Plonk! Plonk! Down came the dung in near perfect circles, each one less full than the one before. The smell was fresh and

131

the dung held the heat of the cow's body for a while after it hit the hard rocky path and sprawled into a lovely shaped cake, a cake that had fallen slightly in the middle and that still held the rings made by the spoon when the fruit was being folded in.

John gave Daisy the tip of the stick to remind her to move on, that toiletries were finished with, but he took note of where the cow dung dropped, as Mary would want to know. The dung would be safe there for a few days—the bluebottles and the horseflies would have to have their share of the spoils before any further action could be taken. He looked up at the sky. Yes, a red sky at night is a farmer's delight.

Next morning as he drove Daisy to the field behind the hill he noted the progress of the cow dung. It was well set with a healthy crust all round it. Yes, it was doing nicely, but it would need another few days. He was afraid that a cart, taking the short cut to the bog, would damage the masterpiece. He ringed a few heavy stones around the dung to ensure that all would be well. His other fear was the weather, the sky was beginning to cloud.

When he had Daisy safely ensconced in the field, he ran back home and returned with three black plastic bags to cover his precious treasures. He tended the cow dung for a week until it lifted from the ground with the ease of a well-baked cake. He put the three dung cakes carefully into the plastic bags and brought them triumphantly home. How to get them into the house was his next move. He knew that his mother would be doing the First Fridays and that he would be left in charge of the house to mind Mary. Yes, that would give him an hour and a half. He hid the three cakes of cow dung at the corner of the haystack and marked the spot with small stones in the shape of a cross.

As soon as his mother left to go to Mass on Friday, he raced outside and brought the presents to the back room where Mary was kept. He never remembered her being anywhere else except in that room. She sat there swaying from side to side, staring at a faraway object. His mother said that she was praying to the angels.

He knew that when he brought her the dung, there would be a quieting down as she took each hard caked piece of dung and crumbled it to pieces. The dry smell had a way of calming her as she played with it and threw it into the air. Then he waited for the moment and it always happened, her eyes would light on John and a strange earthy gaze would come upon her. He knew that she was a *duine le Dia*.

> (Moya notes that *duine le Dia* means in Irish "a person with God.")

Where to Get Help for Writing in Other Forms

There is not enough space in this book to go as deeply as I would like into forms other than poetry and fiction. There are excellent resources for these forms. Those I have found most helpful are the following:

Playwriting

Go to the theater. There is no substitute for live performance to learn what is possible, what works and what does not work on stage. The best published resources I have found are publications of the Dramatists Guild, 234 West 44th Street, New York, NY 10036. A subscription to their newsletter brings with it their journals, which are packed with helpful information about the craft of playwriting and markets. Good libraries will probably have back issues.

Songwriting

Judd Waldin, the composer whose distinguished career in musical theater includes his score for *Raisin*, the Tony Award–winning Best Musical of 1974 based on Lorraine Hansberry's *A Raisin in the Sun,* cites Sheila Davis's workshops at the New School in New York City and her books on songwriting as the best resources available to songwriters today.

In regard to musical theater, both Judd and I participate in the BMI Lehman Engel Musical Theater Workshops led by Maury Yeston (whose credits include *Nine* and *Grand Hotel*) and Susan Schulman (*The Secret Garden*). For information about these and other musical theater workshops, write Norma Grossman, Director, BMI Lehman Engel Musical Theater Workshop, 320 West 57th Street, New York, NY 10019.

Screenwriting

The best books written to help the screenwriter are Linda Seger's *Making A Good Script Great, Creating Unforgettable Characters,* and *The Art of Adaptation: Turning Fact and Fiction into Film.*

Nonfiction

An excellent beginning place for the nonfiction writer is the compendium of articles by leading nonfiction writers in *The Complete Guide to Writing Non-Fiction* by the American Society of Journalists and Authors, edited by Glen Evans.

A WORD OF CAUTION

In all genres of writing, those books, articles, seminars, or workshops that preach a negative, defeatist message are not helpful. I once opened a book on screenwriting in which a successful playwright took many pages to tell me that I really don't stand a chance; getting into the Screenwriter's Guild is too hard, there are too many people trying already, and so on. A book like that is poison to the creative writer. We don't need it! There is always room for excellent work, and there are always generous people who will help the beginner find his or her way. If the book you begin to read discourages you, stop reading it.

PART TWO

Writing with Others

CHAPTER SEVEN

WRITING WITH OTHERS:
WHY AND HOW TO BEGIN

There is a revolution under way in the teaching of writing. It was begun by Peter Elbow in his book *Writing without Teachers* and has been continued by gifted teachers in so many places it now has a name: the Writing Process Movement. My work is within the stream of that movement. I offer a complete model for writing groups and workshops, developed at Amherst Writers & Artists (AWA), tested over many years, and found to be effective in a wide variety of contexts.

I have led workshops in my own living room, in college and graduate school classrooms, in low-income housing projects, in a care center for pregnant teenagers, in a convent in Ireland, and in a retreat center in Japan. Others whom I have trained have in turn led workshops in their own living rooms as well as in prisons, in homes for the elderly, in elementary and high schools, among hospice volunteers, and in a remarkable experiment that brought together mainstream high school students and students who were Cambodian refugees.

In the AWA workshop model the way of the writer is respected as unique to each individual. One person cannot tell another how to write, what to learn next, when to break free of fear and learned constraints. Nevertheless, a context—a community—is created in which the individual writer is strengthened, supported, and enabled to find his or her own way. People writing together in a supportive group not only dramatically improve in craft and in confidence, they also create bonds of profound understanding.

In this book and in *Tell Me Something I Can't Forget,* the Florentine documentary film about my workshop for women in housing projects, I suggest a methodology for writing workshops that minimizes hierarchy and maximizes native human wisdom, that restores confidence in the brilliance of the particular human voice as it is used on the street, in the shop, in the bedroom and kitchen. In these workshops, writers are discovering that *supportive community is the setting in which truly great writing can most easily and effectively happen.*

The AWA model is described with illustrative stories in this chapter and the one that follows. If you are already leading or participating in a writing workshop or if you want to establish such a group, you will find suggestions, exercises, and stories to help you form and sustain a healthy community of writers. If you are a solitary writer, perhaps you will find a kind of community in these stories, exercises, and samples drawn from the lives and work of other writers.

WRITING WITH OTHERS CAN HELP YOU

Writing together in AWA-style workshops has proven to be of great assistance to poets, playwrights, fiction writers, newspaper reporters, songwriters, nonfiction writers, and so on. Some of the benefits are addressed below.

Believe in Your Own Art

It is sad that so often teachers and professors in writing classes, groups, and workshops concentrate on "criticism"—telling students what is "wrong" in their writing. Most of us already believe in our own weaknesses. What we need to hear is our ability, our facility, the effectiveness and strength of our own peculiar and inimitable voices.

In an AWA workshop, people write together and read aloud to one another work that they have just written and have not had time to revise nor even read over to themselves. This is a powerful and often emotional experience, both for the writer and for the reader. Other members of the group do not make any critical comments or suggestions for revision of that new work; they respond only by mentioning what they like and what they remember. This is crucial protection at a critical point in the creation of a new work.

Perhaps the most revolutionary aspect of this workshop method is the absolute insistence that there be a safe place in which to experiment, explore, journey into dangerous internal terrain in one's writing. That safe place depends totally upon knowing that in the moments following your creation of new work, there will be no critique.

This is not a popular belief. We have been so acclimated to a competitive, football-field attitude toward all endeavors, it is difficult to get rid of the idea that the "real writer has to be able to take it on the chin." Which can mean that authentic response to creative work is violent. Hundreds of writers in AWA workshops have proven that there is another way, a way that produces a high percentage of works of art, awarded prizes, work published, produced, and recorded, as well as received privately by friends.

Most of us understand instinctively how to encourage and assist a child to do creative work. If a child brings you a picture she has just drawn with a blue crayon of a bird in flight, and you see that the left wing is hanging awkwardly down the page, but the right wing is soaring, you do not say, "By the way, you've got a crooked left wing there." You say, "Oh, look! Look at that wonderful right wing, how it is lifted in the air! I can just *feel* the flying!" The child looks at the picture and goes back to her crayon and fixes the left wing so it, too, soars.

We know this about children, but in classrooms everywhere, young people and adults are subjected to the opposite treatment in response to their creative work. There is no difference in this matter between the artist at age 4 and the artist at age 54. The artist in me learns best by having my strengths affirmed and will die if I am given a regular dose of criticism at the moments of my greatest vulnerability—that is, immediately following the creation of new work. My own vision of what I am trying to do must be kept clean and clear of the opinions of others until I have had an opportunity to revise my work. Otherwise, it can be destroyed.

There is a time and a place for criticism, revision, editing. A community of writers can be of vast assistance to one another in these matters. But that time is after the writer has had an opportunity to rework his or her first draft and asks for a critical response. Before the work is in manuscript form, there should be no criticism offered. When the time comes for critique, it should be honest and thorough, but balanced with affirmation of what is already working well.

In this kind of group you will grow as a writer, not only in craft but in what is even more essential—belief in your own art.

Learn Craft

In a writing group, what one person learns can become a lesson for all. When one member of a workshop struggles to reduce the number of adjectives in a paragraph, all the members learn the danger of using too many adjectives. When one member has written brilliant dialogue and the group talks together about how natural and unique is each character's speech, all the members of the workshop are studying dialogue.

Have Support in Taking Risks

Each time one member of a workshop tries something new, all the other members are invited by that risk-taking to try new forms, break old taboos, write with increased courage. Sharing your writing with others and listening to the writing of others can give you courage to take greater risks, to tell deeper truth, to trust your own instincts. Writing with others can strengthen your nerve.

Correct Mistakes

It can be invaluable to have another writer read your writing and tell you in a caring way if and how your work leaves her or him confused, unconvinced, or dissatisfied. Questions and suggestions can be offered in a tone that does not assume superiority. Complete honesty and thoroughness in critique, and the necessity of revision, do not have to mean humiliation and embarrassment for the writer.

Know About Publication Possibilities

Writing with others can help you to know when and where to send a manuscript for publication. Your writing companions can give you examples and encouragement.

A writing group gives you a place in which to gain perspective and support when you are overwhelmed by rejections, and a place in which to celebrate accomplishments. In my workshops I frequently ask if anyone has received a rejection slip. I often read my own out loud in the session. We celebrate rejection slips as evidence that the writer is keeping his or her work out; we groan together, laugh, console.

We all experience victory when an acceptance comes to one of us. We correct each other when someone talks about "submitting" a manuscript, remembering Marge Piercy's advice, "Never 'submit'! Offer."

Don Fisher, a poet and playwright in my Amherst workshop, received the following rejection letter from a Canadian journal, *Dead Tree Product*. One of the poems it refers to, "A Poem About Love and Astronomy," appears in Exercise 32.

Dear Don Fisher:

Thanks for your poems. I really disliked "A Poem About Love and Astronomy," and I liked the other two enough, moreso "A Bit of Conversation..." due to the strength of the image. But it doesn't really matter, because Dead Tree Product *has folded due to financial difficulties. Sorry for this inconvenience.*

Good luck writing. Thanks for your material. I liked the Laurel and Hardy stamps, but, you fool, U.S. stamps in Canada are like Canadian money in the States...pretty worthless. Nice try. Buy an IRC next time.

I apologize again for the inconvenience.
Gabino Vidal Travassos
ex-fiction editor
Dead Tree Product

The lively time we had talking about at this rejection eased the sting of it for Don and reminded all of us to buy IRCs when offering work to Canadian journals.

Network

By meeting together, writers form important relationships that result in collaborations, in taking group action when some injustice has been done to one of their members, and in making contacts with editors, agents, and other professionals.

Complete the Artistic Act

Writing is an act of communication. As writer/artist, when you read your work to someone else or allow it to be read, you give your art into the mind of your reader or listener. It is received; you have communicated. You have done the work of the artist.

Heal Inner Wounds

Although this belief is not popular in some circles, I believe writing is inextricably linked to working on one's own inner life and outer relationships. Writing is communication, and the crucible in which it occurs is community. I don't care whether it is in the highest university or the lowest prison, any writing group in which one person is arrogantly judging others is sick. A healthy writing group is a healthy community, and to participate in it, whether the goal is publication or healing, is to be a more healthy human being.

WRITING WITH OTHERS: SOME OPTIONS

The loneliness of the writer is legendary. Who has not seen images of the starving artist (usually a male) bent over a typewriter with a glass of strong liquor as his only companion? This stereotype is not only false, it is dangerous. Not all great writers are antisocial alcoholics, half-mad eccentrics, or suicidally depressed. Some have been; some are. But there are many who live quite happy lives, and being in communication with other writers can make the chances greater that your own writing life will be a happy one. The following are some options.

Forming a Partnership with Another Writer

For many writers, the first step in writing with others is to find one other writer with whom to talk about the work you both are doing. This may or may not include writing together; it may be simply sharing writing that each of you has done separately.

Finding a person to be your primary writing companion is somewhat like finding a good doctor, a good therapist, a good priest, or a good life partner, but it is worth the effort. Family members and close nonwriter friends are not usually good candidates. They care too much, want too badly to please or correct us, have different versions of our stories, recognize our source material, and for all kinds of reasons are usually the very last folks we should ask to be our writing partners.

Perhaps the best place to find a writing companion is in a writing workshop or class. Many people who have participated in my workshops become friends with other members and eventually gather informally in each other's homes for the sharing and response they need.

Joining a Writing Workshop

In most areas there are groups of writers who work together in a support group or workshop. Although my model of workshop encourages writers to work in various forms, many workshops focus on one genre only. You can locate these through your library or your local school system or college.

Writing groups are sometimes offered in newspapers to the public free of charge. This advantage is balanced by the disadvantage that the skill and energy of wise, experienced leadership doesn't usually come gratis, and if it does, it is usually a closed membership among friends.

There are several things to remember in choosing a workshop for which there is a fee. Remember that you are the consumer, the purchaser, of a service, whether the "vendor" is Harvard University or your next-door neighbor. In most university and college workshops there is an evaluation period during which you can change your mind and get most of your tuition back. You should be able to do this with a private workshop as well.

Most workshops are led by people who are either published writers or have completed a Master of Fine Arts degree in creative writing. An MFA means that the person who has received it has some knowledge of other writers and has written work that passed an academic committee. He or she may or may not be a good teacher, may or may not be insightful, sensitive, helpful to other writers. There are also gifted teachers and excellent workshop leaders without these credentials.

When you find a writing group or workshop, ask if you may visit once, either for a fee or as a guest. Ask if after three meetings you may choose to drop out and receive a refund for the remainder of your tuition. After the third meeting, make up your own mind on the basis of this test: when I go home from the meeting, do I feel more like writing—or less like writing? This is the only test that matters, no matter how famous the leader, no matter how impressive the format, no matter how much you want to believe otherwise. What is important is that you understand what you need, and do not feel that what you need is less courageous or less valid, less mature, or less artistically appropriate than what some other writer needs. Even that method which is most destructive to one person may energize and challenge another person. The professor or group leader who uses sarcasm and put-down while destroying the confidence of one student may cause another student's adrenaline to rise, and in an attitude of "I'll be goddamed if I'm going to be destroyed by this (bleep)," great writing may happen.

Starting Your Own Writing Group

If you cannot find a workshop or writing group that meets your needs, start your own. If you feel that your own experience as a writer, teacher, or workshop leader is adequate, call the group a workshop, follow your own experience and the guidelines offered in this book and elsewhere, and lead it yourself.

When I first started leading a workshop in my own hometown, it seemed a very arrogant thing to do; after all, my community already boasted five colleges, each with its own writing program. But I had something to offer that the big institutions were not offering: an intimate community of writers meeting not for an academic degree, but simply to help each other write. That first workshop has grown to an organization that has had as many as 12 workshops for adults, children, and youth, led by eight leaders in five towns. As Amherst Writers & Artists, we have established a press, published 12 issues of *Peregrine* (a national literary journal), nine volumes of poetry, and an anthology of the writings of women in low-income housing projects in western Massachusetts. What we have done is possible in almost any community.

If you do not have much experience writing and/or publishing, but are skilled in group dynamics and can creatively and effectively lead a group, then call it a writers support group and see yourself as the group facilitator. Allow knowledge about writing and publishing to arise from the members themselves as you study and work together. I recommend that you charge a modest fee if you see yourself as administrator alone, and a more substantial fee if you are also skilled in writing and teaching.

Even if you do not feel you have any of the skills above, you may want to meet with one or more friends and, without a leader, just follow the guidelines in the next chapter and do the exercises that follow. A writer is someone who writes; a writing group can simply be several writers who meet together and share their wisdom and their kindness.

144

How to Begin a Workshop
or Writing Group

Many of the lessons I learned "by guess and by gosh," as my grandmother used to say, *you* do not have to learn the hard way. Answer the questions below, step by step, and follow the guidelines. They will help you to avoid many of the pitfalls I could not foresee, since I began my writing groups without any appropriate models to follow.

Decide What Kind of Group You Want

1. Who will the members be?

Will you invite both men and women? I have two workshops each week for both men and women, and one for women only. Unfortunately, I cannot offer one for men only, since I am a woman, but I think such an opportunity would be a fine thing. Some people are more creative in mixed groups, some do best among their own gender. Some want to write with a focus on only one genre or in a context of other people with shared life experience. The last section of this chapter, "If You Are Planning a Group for Special Membership," offers some suggestions. The decision about your kind of group should be based on your own interest and comfort as leader.

Will you invite only experienced writers, or include beginners? In my experience, it is best to mix experienced and inexperienced writers together. Some of the freshest, strongest writers I have worked with come free of preconceptions about what "literature" is. And some of the wisest, kindest workshop members have been those who have written and published widely, are willing to share their experience, and are able to receive encouragement and support from others. A wide variety of people in a workshop gives a writer a rich range of responses to his or her work.

Will you require a writing sample before admitting someone to the workshop? I never do. The work that writers will do in a supportive group is almost always far better than what they have written previously. Also, I don't want to limit my groups to writers who have been handpicked, and I don't want to be prejudiced ahead of time by reading something that may have been written in terror under pressure of receiving a grade. Remember my story of Mary and the children's book in Chapter Six? I would have missed one of my favorite writers if I had tested her by the work she was doing prior to my workshop.

A mixed population—in age, economic and educational level, writing experience, and preferred genre—creates a rich mulch of ideas, forms, and possibilities in the group. Everyone brings some unique gift of life experience and perspective. All writers are strengthened by hearing work in various forms; many beginning writers do not know what they write best; and many experienced writers will surprise themselves by writing in a form they have not tried before. Working in a diversified group helps us to be generous, to share what we know and to learn from everyone else.

2. Will it be a workshop or a sharing group?

Earlier in this section, I presented the distinction in these terms. Decide which definition fits your leadership style. (From this point on, I will use the term *workshop* to mean any creative writing group.)

3. Will your workshop be for only one genre, or will it be open?

I prefer workshops that are not genre-specific; that is, poets and fiction writers, playwrights and librettists, nonfiction writers and songwriters are all mixed together. I myself write in many different forms, and I think it makes writing less arduous, more fun, full of surprise, and ultimately more effective.

4. Decide on meeting place, time, and maximum number of participants.

If you do not have a quiet, spacious area in your own home, you will want to find a comfortable room to rent for the hours of your workshop. See the discussion below under "Prepare a Place."

I suggest a three-hour period for a workshop meeting. Three workshops meet each week in my home on Tuesday, Wednesday, and Thursday evenings from 7:30 to 10:30. Amherst Writers & Artists also offers a three-hour morning workshop, occasional all-day Saturday writing retreats from 9:30 to 4:30 with lunch included, and two full weekend writing retreats each year. Any of these options can be adapted for your workshop.

I suggest 12 as a maximum number of participants. That will give you a good gathering at meetings when several are absent, and when all are present it is still manageable. I suggest that you wait until you have at least five participants before beginning. In the early days I recruited friends to be "warm bodies," coming free of charge until I had enough paying participants to make the group effective.

5. Will you charge tuition? If so, how much?

This decision should be based on two considerations: your own professional level, and the market price for similar services in your community. As a teacher with an MFA in creative writing and years of experience in group work, I base my workshop fee on the amount paid by a special student taking a comparable number of classroom course hours at our area colleges. If you are a leader without academic credentials but with experience in writing and publishing or group work, I advise you to research the cost of comparable services and charge accordingly. This workshop model is equally effective for groups that gather informally with no leader and no tuition.

When you have made these decisions, you are ready to publicize your workshop.

Publicize Your Workshop

You will need three kinds of publicity to begin a new workshop: a poster, a brief community calendar announcement, and a news release. The text of the poster and the calendar announcement are basically the same. My own might read:

Amherst Writers & Artists

CREATIVE WRITING WORKSHOP

Leader: Pat Schneider, MFA

Tuesday evenings, 7:30 P.M.

77 McClellan Street, Amherst

For more information call 413-253-3307

The news release will give more information. Write "For Immediate Release" at the top of your page, the event date, and your name and telephone number as the contact person. Always use full double space, and put the most important information first; newspaper editors like to chop off the ends when they lack sufficient space. Mail your publicity to your local paper, radio stations, libraries, schools and churches. Take copies of the poster to area grocery stores, laundromats, and bus stops. The success of Amherst Writers & Artists in the early days was completely dependent on the hard work done in publicity. Margaret Robison and I began together, which is much easier than beginning alone. We went to our local radio station and volunteered to put on a regular program in which we interviewed area writers (and plugged our workshop!). We talked a local printer into making beautiful posters for the program in exchange for free ads on the radio station, and our feet beat the sidewalks of Amherst and surrounding towns, taking those posters everywhere.

Prepare a Place

Place is important. Some safety, some care must go into its preparation. I prefer to lead workshops in my own home, an old farmhouse near the center of town. We gather in a circle until I have given an exercise, then people spread out into several rooms to write, coming back together for reading that new material and critiquing manuscripts.

When I lead a workshop in an academic setting, I arrive early, arrange the chairs in a circle, put some kind of printed handout material on each chair, and have some refreshments on a side table. (I have seen two studies reporting that generating new writing burns as many calories as running, bicycling, or making love! This is not absurd; the brain uses enormous energy—in fact, one quarter of the body's basal metabolism.)

What to Say When People Call

If you have two or three interested members, tell them you will call them when you have five prospective members (you may invite a couple of friends to attend free until you can fill their spots).

After you have met once with your first five interested people, tell callers that it is possible you may have an opening soon, and they may come once as your guest. This immediately establishes you as a generous and secure person; it also gives you an opportunity to see whether the person is right for your group.

When you have done all that is suggested above, you are ready to open your door and welcome your new workshop members!

If You Are Planning a Group for Special Membership

The workshop model described in the next chapter is based on my regular creative writing workshops; however, you may want to adapt that model to a specialized membership. If so, you will want to make changes appropriate to each group.

For example, in working with women in low-income housing projects, I developed an entirely different way of handling manuscripts than that which is described in Chapter Eight. Most of the women cannot type, and so I take their handwritten pages home and make a little textbook of them consisting of their original copy, a typed copy as they wrote it with my remarks, and a finished copy in beautiful manuscript form. Many times the women have said to me that seeing their own words in print, free of spelling errors, is a life-changing experience.

Other groups, such as the workshops that Rob and Andrea Zucker lead for bereaved parents, dispense with manuscripts altogether and simply use written work as the basis for sharing. The brilliant thing about this method as opposed to a usual group-sharing experience lies in the fact that when we write down our thoughts before sharing, we have an opportunity to express our thoughts and feelings without the distraction of other people's facial expressions, body messages, and so forth. That which we choose to share, then, is a more inner and more personal sharing.

In adapting this model to children, some of whom are as young as third graders, Ani Tuzman finds it helpful to begin each writing session with a quiet time. She rings some gentle chimes and lights a candle to help them center and become ready to write. This poem, by nine-year-old Sarah Kavanagh, was written after such a quiet time:

> I looked for
> the gold
> at the end
> of the rainbow
> that I didn't find.
>
> Nor did I find
> the silver
> at the end of the sky.
>
> But I did find
> the light
> within myself
>
> and the magic
> only I can see.
>
> I looked for myself
> and found
> me.

One of the most interesting adaptations of the workshop model has been a group led by Kathryn Dunn. Half the students in the workshop are mainstream high school students. The other half are ESL (English as a Second

Language) students, mostly Cambodian refugees. Kathy reports that the students write and share their life stories and sometimes are moved to tears from what they learn about one another.

Sophal Chhoun writes of her escape from the Khmer Rouge to bring fish to her starving family and of her return to genocide.

The Moon Light

The light guides her way home
running home under the moon light
escaping from men in black
running across the rice field.

With water and leeches
her foot sinks into the mud
as she makes her moves.

Trying not to make a sound
she tries to move like the wind.
Bringing home a couple of fish in her pocket.

Hiding her body in the rice weed
as the leech sucks blood from her body
into his body.

She says will this light bring me home safe
will this light bring me to death.

As a man in black paces across the road
she digs down
like the crab digging its way into the ground.
The wind hits the rice weed softly.

She creeps like the sound of the wind
but where is she?
Does the light bring her to her mother?
Does the light bring her to her death?

No, the light brings her to her family.

She empties her pocket as her mother's tears
drip by drip.

Running back to the men in black
before the sun rises over the rice field.

I encourage you to turn now to the next chapter, and as you read it, imagine
ways in which you might adapt it to meet your own needs and the needs of
others who can discover that they truly are writer/artists.

KEEPING A WRITERS WORKSHOP HEALTHY

*I*n this chapter I have created a fictional workshop. The 12 workshop members I describe are imagined, created from experiences of my own, combined into composites. All names and characters are fictional with the exception of Eva Brown, who asked that I use her real name and tell her actual story. Each of the 12 members illustrates one suggestion for keeping a workshop healthy.

If you are already a workshop member, you will find familiar problems described and perhaps some new solutions. If you are a workshop leader, the suggestions outlined here will help you to strengthen and maintain a supportive community of writers. If you are a solitary writer, I believe you will enjoy the stories in this chapter and find some useful information for your own writing life.

I am fortunate to have had many different kinds of groups in which to test this workshop model. Recently, as I was working on this book, a letter arrived from Brunswick, Maine, from Anne Dellenbaugh, owner of *Her Wild Song: Wilderness Trips for Women,* listing all the equipment I need to bring for the wilderness canoe trip she will lead, and the writing workshop I will lead this summer on the West branch of the Penobscot River. I am in my fifties and have never been on a canoe trip! I am excited and a little frightened about this opportunity; that's why I want to do it. Adapting the workshop to new circumstances always brings a new surge of energy and stirs up new writing in me, as well as evoking it from my workshop participants.

I invite you to adapt these suggestions to the particular needs of your own group. You will find yourself and others growing rapidly in craft and in confidence.

Conducting a Healthy Workshop Meeting

Before introducing the workshop members who will illustrate suggestions for a healthy workshop, let me list the suggestions themselves in summary fashion. Here's how to ensure that the group will be of great significance to your writers, and at the same time be truly supportive:

How to Keep a Workshop Healthy—12 Suggestions:

1. Invite, but do not pressure, members to read what they have just written in the workshop.
2. Do not allow the workshop to critique or correct work that has just been written in the workshop.
3. Allow great diversity in age, experience, style, and genre in your workshop.
4. Assume all written work to be fictional unless the writer volunteers that it is autobiographical.
5. Encourage workshop members to be honest with both praise and critical suggestion in responding to work in manuscript form.
6. Give your workshop a wide variety of exercises.
7. Write along with your workshop members, read that work aloud, and invite response.
8. If one person is making the group unworkable, ask that person to leave.
9. Do not be thrown off center by anyone else's expertise; be realistic about your own.
10. In moments of genuine crisis, be ready to abandon all rules.
11. Help people try out new forms.
12. Stress confidentiality.

MEET THE WORKSHOP MEMBERS

It is Thursday evening, almost 7:30. I have prepared a place; there are 12 comfortable chairs arranged in a circle. The house smells of chocolate. On the kitchen table are hot coffee and tea and a plate of brownies. There is also a dish of carrot and celery sticks. Beside them, I have laid out an array of announcements, several literary journals that are advertising for manuscripts, the latest copies of *Poets and Writers,* the *Dramatists Guild Newsletter,* the *American Poetry Review,* and the *Associated Writing Programs Newsletter.* There is a copy of the *Directory of Literary Magazines* compiled by the Council of Literary Magazines and Presses. There is a looseleaf notebook full of guidelines from journals, and a folder of current contest announcements.

The first four people to arrive at this imagined workshop are the most inexperienced in the group.

Jeanne, Inexperienced and Afraid

The first person to arrive is Jeanne, who is the mother of four children, a woman who left high school without finishing and never went back. She has always wanted to write but is frightened of spelling and punctuation and grammar and is insecure about her West Virginia accent. She is certain that everyone else is far more accomplished than she is and has come to the workshop only on the strength of great courage.

Jeanne does not know she will do her most powerful writing about her family in a coal mining town, the baths she took as a child standing, shivering, in a galvanized tub near the wood stove, the struggles of those who wanted to form a union.

For many weeks Jeanne has not read anything to us, but she has been writing in her notebook, and when I have asked her how she's doing, she says, "I'm okay, but I'm not ready to read anything yet." I have told her she may remain silent as long as she wants and I have encouraged her to begin by writing about her childhood. Tonight, for the first time, Jeanne will take the risk of reading, and for the first time she will hear others telling her

155

what they like and what they remember. She will go home with her confidence strengthened, and her voice a bit more free.

> *Suggestion 1: Invite, but do not pressure, members to read what they have just written in the workshop.* Only in an atmosphere of utmost safety can language flow freely. I believe that people can be trusted to know when it is safe to read and when it is better to remain silent.

Eva, Whose Native Tongue Is Not English

The next person to arrive is Eva Brown, who has generously given permission for her story to be included here. Eva was born in Germany in 1938 and heard only the German language spoken until she was four months old, when her family fled to France and stopped speaking German entirely, fearing they would be sent to concentration camps. Eva heard only French spoken for the next two and a half years. At age three her family moved to New York City and spoke English, although she thinks her father probably still spoke German at home. Eva works as a psychologist and writes professional documents. She wants to learn to write in a way that is more creative, less formal. She feels overwhelmed by the ease and freedom others seem to have in their writing. Eva's written work seems always to have a slightly heightened formality, as if there were a trace of accent that you cannot quite identify. She does not yet guess that the voice in which she speaks will be exactly right to tell the stories of her displacement by war, which are her deepest resource. To Eva and to all writers whose native language is not English, I always extend encouragement to write their first draft in their mother tongue. If Eva writes in the language that comes most naturally to her she may recover memories, knowledge, and freedom that seem to have been lost to her.

> *Suggestion 2: Do not allow the workshop to critique or correct work that has just been written in the workshop.* Writing that has just come from the pen of a writer should not be critiqued by

156

other people. A piece of writing, newly born, is as fragile and raw as a newborn baby, and should be treated as respectfully, as tenderly. When my workshop members write together side by side and read that new work to one another, I do not allow anyone to make overt or subtle suggestions for change. What is helpful is giving back to the writer what the listener remembers and what the listener likes.

Andy, Who Is Young

The next workshop member to arrive is Andy, a junior in high school. He comes on a bicycle, wearing a huge plastic helmet and a backpack. He writes science fiction, amazes us with his constant invention, never finishes anything, and wants more than anything in the world to be a writer. Andy is a great asset to the group. His energy and inventive imagination are good for us all. He will write for several years in my workshop, and he will resist my every effort to get him to bring anything in on paper to hand out for workshop response. For four years I will allow this, encourage him, tell him my honest delight in the incredible worlds he creates and reads aloud to us. Then there will come a day when I will say to him, "Now, Andrew. It is time for you to be sending manuscripts out to literary journals." I will set deadlines, and Andy's work will begin to be published.

Suggestion 3: Allow for great diversity in age, experience, style, and genre in your workshop. It breaks down competitiveness, increases compassion, and allows more learning to happen in everyone. The elderly writer learns from the slang of the young; the young writer learns from the experience of the old. The sophisticated writer is given courage to be plain and earthy; the plain and earthy writer is enabled to write with sophistication. The skilled writer teaches the unskilled about form; the unskilled writer invites the skilled writer to trust his or her own instincts.

Faye, Whose Subject Matter Is Controversial

Faye is in her late twenties, dresses in jeans, T-shirt, and sneakers, and writes graphic first-person stories about life as a prostitute in a neighboring town. She writes in first person about johns and one-night stands and fear of AIDS. No one in the group knows whether Faye's work is fiction or autobiography. A retired public health nurse in the workshop tells me I should privately ask Faye questions, offer counsel. With some inner ambivalence, I say no, that is not what Faye wants from me; if she did, she would ask. I tell the nurse to follow her own instincts, if she feels like intervening. I feel it is my task to protect Faye's boundaries by providing her with a good workshop and a safe place to speak the truth of her life and of her imagination.

Faye will write her stories and listen to us tell her what we like and what we remember. She will receive our comments on the pages of her manuscripts. Then, suddenly, she will disappear from my workshop. From my life. And I will feel grief, and I will always wonder how she is, where she is. But I am not a therapist or a social worker or a minister. Whether her work is fiction or autobiography is irrelevant to the strength of her writing. Fiction is just another way to tell the truth.

Suggestion 4: Assume all written work to be fictional unless the writer volunteers that it is autobiographical. Even if the writer is moved to tears as he or she reads, respond to the written work by saying, "The narrator...the child...the mother..." and so forth, rather than "You...your grandmother...your lover." In *Tell Me Something I Can't Forget,* the documentary about my workshop with low-income women, there is a scene in which Robin Therrian breaks down as she reads about the suicide of her mother when Robin was a child. We wait in silence as she struggles to read. When she cannot, I offer to read for her. When she says no, I say, "Okay. Now. We're a writing workshop, and we love each other. But the way we protect each other is to deal with this as writing. So what can we say about what we've been given in the piece of writing? What's strong? What stays with you?" The workshop members slowly and carefully name images that moved us, and Robin listens.

Your task as workshop leader is to protect the writer by keeping the boundaries clear. I always discourage responses that begin "That makes me think of the time when..." The sharing of related experiences by other members of the workshop moves attention away from what has been written and disappoints the writer by removing the focus from discussion of his or her manuscript.

I am convinced that only when all work is given the dignity of being treated as literature, as separate from the life story of the writer, can a group of writers be truly free to write about anything. This is always awkward at first—some people find it easier to do than others, and the leader has to give gentle reminders— but it keeps the discussion on track and prevents digression into personal exchanges that are not centered on the written work.

The workshop room is filling up on this imaginary Thursday evening. People leave their note pads on their favorite chairs and go to the kitchen table to get a cup of coffee and a brownie.

The next four persons to arrive are more experienced writers.

George's Attitude Gets in the Way

George is a medical doctor working on a novel. When he first joined the workshop, George could not seem to write beyond one or two paragraphs before something seemed to stop him. I didn't understand why this was happening and was at a loss to help him. It was another member of the workshop who said one evening, "You know, George, every time you read to us, it is short, just about the length of a doctor's medical dictation." The look on George's face was pure revelation. The very next time he wrote, the block was dissolved, and the novel had begun.

George has trouble writing about women. When he writes about an emergency procedure in the operating room, the work is intensely interesting, fresh, believable. But when he tries to write about women, everything goes flat. He has two women in the novel; he refers to them as "the fair Jeanette" and "the ravishing Nona." The fair Jeanette has blond hair and bright blue eyes that are always "twinkling." The ravishing Nona has black hair and black eyes that are always "snapping." Neither woman has a wrinkle, a blemish, a wart, a hair out of place. George knows he has a problem here; he is shy, and working on this part of his writing is very difficult for him.

As I sit trying to find a way to help him, I remember the traumatic experience I had in graduate school when my professor, Andrew Fetler, told me flatly that my writing was terrible. His words float into my mind: "The problem is not with the way you write. It's with the way you think."

As is so often true with teaching, suddenly I realize I am learning—for the first time I really understand what Andy was trying to tell me. For the first time I can accept that he was right, even though it was terribly hard for me to hear.

I tell George the story: how I was so angry I dared in a white heat to tell my own story, the real truth in all its complexity and confusion, in order to prove to my teacher that there was another way of thinking in me, a way that he had not seen on the page. George looks at me and smiles. "What you're asking me to do is change my life," he says.

We are silent for a moment, and then I say, "George, that's what writing does to all of us. That's one reason why it's so scary. It shows us how we think."

George says he has to work on the way he thinks about women. Until that changes, he can't write about them in a way that will satisfy a reader (with the possible exception of readers who share his point of view!). I ask why all the doctors are called "Doctor Brown" and "Doctor Filmore" while all the nurses and secretaries are called "Sally" and "Anne." He tells me, "I can't do anything about the doctors. That's not my problem. That's the way it really is in a hospital."

Suggestion 5: Encourage workshop members to be honest with
both praise and critical suggestion in responding to work in

manuscript form. Every writer has prejudices, blind spots, inadequacies. If the narrator's attitude in the written text is sexist or racist, ageist or classist, acknowledgment of that fact will help the writer. Every writer makes mistakes and typos, is sometimes vague, awkward, or derivative. Getting back 12 copies of your manuscript with all those things marked is of great assistance to any writer. I suggest to workshop members that they read manuscripts twice, first noting anything that stops or disrupts their reading, then in the second reading noting what they particularly liked. It is important to balance a critical response.

Joan Writes for Fun

Joan is a weaver, a member of the town government, active in her local Quaker meetings. Writing has always been easy for Joan. She loves language, is a natural storyteller, and writes for the fun of it. She has a collection of manuscripts: short stories, poems, three novels, and several plays. She wants help in beginning to publish.

Joan is one of the few writers I have known who "writes" an entire book in her head (sometimes almost instantaneously) before committing a word to the page. This is unusual. Most writers, like myself, don't have any idea where a piece of writing is going; it reveals itself as it goes along. But Joan always knows the ending before she writes the beginning.

Her strength is in plotting. She is a natural storyteller; suspense seems to be instinctive in her talking and in her writing. But the back side of our strength is almost always our weakness: Joan needs to slow down, allow complexity of character to develop, allow moments of silence to occur. In her introduction to *The Best American Short Stories, 1983,* Anne Tyler says, "Almost every really lasting story—*almost,* you notice—contains at least one moment of stillness that serves as a kind of pivot." When Joan slows down, she will discover that there are poetic moments of stillness in her as well as driving, electric plots.

Suggestion 6: Give your workshop a wide variety of exercises.
This will enable you to evoke each writer's strengths and address each one's weaknesses. Try exercises that will bring poetry into prose writing, and narrative into poetry. Encourage experimentation; invite people to "play." I often remind my writers that visual artists sketch: a finger here, an ear there, and sometimes nothing in between. I tell them that to write in a workshop is to make an artist's sketch.

Surprise is a major factor in exercises. When I bring objects, I keep them hidden in a paper bag until the moment when people are ready to write, and then I don't allow them to talk after I reveal the objects. A man's shaving brush may cause one person to write a funny account of the first time he tried to shave, and may evoke deep grief in another who remembers the death of a father.

Maria Disbelieves Her Work Has Merit

Maria is in her seventies. She has been a hospital administrator and a physician's wife and is now retired and lives alone. She has written and published professional articles. Always dressed up, she writes fiction elegantly and frequently tears up all of her manuscripts. She does not believe her own gifts, which are great. If someone suggests that one of her short stories be offered to a literary journal for publication, Maria laughs and says, "Aren't you *nice!*"

Maria has always wanted to write, but she is instinctively very competitive. She needs to succeed. Under a mask of bravado and good cheer, she is terrified of being embarrassed, terrified of failure. She asks the workshop for severe critiques, but she responds to even gentle critical suggestions by deciding that her work is "shit." Maria's work is witty, urbane, sophisticated, and wise. She is a private woman; her writing carefully conceals her own life.

She will be astonished that I reveal in public my rejection slips; that I say truthfully I am frightened to read brand-new writing aloud; that the writing life continues to be risky. I will tell her how a writer whose book won a Pulitzer Prize and headed the best-seller list for a long time told me that he was completely traumatized at the thought of trying to write another book.

"How can I ever hope to equal what I've already done?" he wailed. I will say that was the moment when I recognized that the fear I felt about my own writing would never go away, no matter how many successes might come.

I hope that Maria will gradually realize she is not alone in her fear and will dare to join me in the risky business of sending our work out for possible publication.

> *Suggestion 7: Write along with your workshop members, read that work aloud, and invite response.* Model for your workshop the truth of the writing life. To do so will be liberating for them and for you also. I take the same risks I am asking my workshop members to take. I write along with them in every writing time, and I try to write courageously. I read autobiographical work of my own sometimes. Every session I read my work aloud at least once, even when it doesn't please me. When I feel afraid to read, I tell them so. Once in each 10-week session I give my workshop members a manuscript of my new writing to critique. I do not take workshop time to discuss my manuscript, but I ask them to write their comments and return the manuscripts to me. Often, when I receive a rejection slip, I read it aloud and invite others to do the same. When I have a triumph, I talk about the details of publishing contracts, agent percentages, promotional appearances. In other words, I take my workshop members in, make them my writing peers. And they are; in this kind of atmosphere success abounds.

Phyllis, Not a Good Group Member

In my 15 years of leading creative writing workshops, there have been many small, human, sometimes comical problems: Someone who falls asleep and snores resoundingly during writing times; someone who chews gum and pops it loudly; someone who smells bad; someone who sits with a skirt hiked up so far the people sitting across from her are embarrassed; someone who comes late every time; someone who leaves early every time; someone who is a therapist and doesn't want to be in a workshop with a client, and on and on. There have been several people who have left because personalities—my own included—did not really connect creatively. Once a woman left because she was offended when I read as a writing exercise the first sexual fantasy in Nancy Friday's *My Secret Garden,* and once a man left because I refused his invitation to take the whole workshop skinny-dipping in a local hot tub!

Only twice have I had to ask someone to leave. One was a man who was so defensive he saw even my *compliments* as an attack on his writing, his manhood, his mother's great-aunt Sarah. The other was a woman whom I shall call Phyllis.

Phyllis had been leading a writing workshop in a neighboring town and called to ask if she might come once as my guest. I said I would be pleased to have her visit. When she arrived she brought with her two other women whom I was not expecting. That evening, one of my writing exercises was to play a portion of a beautiful recording of wild wolves howling. At the end of the evening, Phyllis took me aside and told me that it was irresponsible of me to play the sound of wolves; I might upset people too much. She wanted to join the workshop, however, and since I had an opening, I said she could join.

From the beginning, Phyllis could not live within the "rules of order" I tried to maintain. She would not—could not—keep from telling people what was wrong with their writing, although I explained again and again that we wait until work is in manuscript, we do not critique first draft. Forty-five minutes after we finished responding to someone's work, Phyllis would interrupt whatever discussion was going on, almost always beginning "I just have to say..." and would attack a work we had finished discussing.

Finally I told her I needed to refund her money and ask her not to come back. That was one of the hardest acts I have ever done. My own regret was eased somewhat when Phyllis told me, "It's all right. I've talked to my sister about you, and she told me what's wrong. In a former life, I was your mother, and you have a problem with authority."

Suggestion 8: If one person is making the group unworkable, ask that person to leave. Your responsibility to the group—to keep it

164

healthy, to protect it—may necessitate your asking someone to leave. The bottom line is that you, as a workshop leader, have to be able to work with the people who have gathered. If you can't work with someone, you have a right and a responsibility to protect yourself as well as the group.

Now more than half of my composite workshop has arrived. People are checking books out of my library, looking over the sample journals I have on display, checking the latest submission invitations in *Poets and Writers* and the *A WP Newsletter*.

The last four members to arrive are my most experienced writers.

Amy, an Acclaimed Writer

Amy is a writer whose plays and short stories have received critical acclaim. She teaches writing at a college in a neighboring state and drives two hours each way to attend the workshop. She is one of the funniest writers I have ever had in a workshop; her dry wit makes every session a party for those who come. Amy comes to the workshop because she finds it a stimulating focus for her week of writing. The writing she does in response to exercises I offer becomes the germinating center of short stories, plays, poems. When her play wins a national prize and is performed halfway across the nation, she brings a video of the performance and we set up a separate evening for the viewing. Afterward, we talk about playwriting, and the next week another workshop member begins to write a scene for a play.

Suggestion 9: Do not be thrown off center by anyone else's expertise; be realistic about your own. If we lead our groups without pretension, being open about what we know and what we don't know, we can welcome the participation of very experienced writers. I have at this time in my workshop a physician named Tom Plaut whose books on asthma have sold more than 100,000 copies. Tom certainly does not need my help in knowing how to write medical books! However, in the workshop I provide a community of writers where he experiments with new forms and shares his wisdom in the areas of his own expertise.

Connie, a Writer Who Is Suffering

Connie is a beautiful young woman who has been in the workshop for several years. She is a brilliant poet, has published two books of poetry, and is regularly published in literary journals. During the course of the workshop, Connie discovers that her four-year-old child has leukemia. The child is dying over a period of months, and Connie goes through denial, rage, grief. She cannot write about anything else. Often, as she reads her written work, Connie weeps.

Another member of the workshop comes to me complaining. He suggests that I refer her to a therapist and ask her to leave the workshop. I refuse to do this. I tell him that Connie's subject, like all of our subjects, really "chooses" her, and in every other respect her participation in the workshop is comfortable; she responds sensitively to the work of others. I try to tell him gently that if he finds it too uncomfortable and needs to leave I will refund the remainder of his tuition. He does choose to leave.

Soon after Connie's child dies, she becomes pregnant again, goes through a brief period of joy, and then loses the pregnancy in the third month. She is inconsolable. She writes one evening in workshop that her mother, with whom she has a difficult relationship, has said, "Why in the world don't you just forget it? That fetus wasn't any bigger than a nickel!"

This time my own heart feels broken. The workshop is made of 12 people who have been together for a long time. We have listened to Connie's images of nature, her joy in the natural world before the illness of her child and the loss of her baby. Now the cruel insensitivity of her mother feels like too much. Suddenly I know that the workshop is more than a workshop to Connie, and to all of us. It is a community. We are companions; we are in this moment even family.

I ask Connie if it would feel good to her for us to have a little ceremony for the lost baby. I say that if she would like, we will all sing a lullaby and then, since it is a simple and natural thing for me to do, I will pray for the

166

journey of the child. She nods her head. In my voice that is good only for lullabies, I begin, "Sleep, my baby, peace attend thee, all through the night..." The workshop joins, we sing the song quietly, gently. And then I pray a simple blessing on the life and on the journey of the baby.

> *Suggestion 10: In moments of genuine crisis, be ready to abandon all rules.*

Michael, Who Wants to Try a Different Genre

Michael is an engineer whose book on designing bridges has sold out in three editions and has been translated into Spanish and Japanese. He is working on a second, related book, and already has a contract for its publication. Michael's mother died this spring, and the farmhouse in which he grew up was put up for auction. Images have been coming up that don't fit into his bridge books. He brings me several short journal entries about the barn, the tools, the hired man, the jersey cow, the spider in the corner of the haymow. "What do I do with these?" he wants to know.

> *Suggestion 11: Help people try out new forms.* Often the need to move from one form to another is the source of a writer's block. To try poetry may seem "pretentious"; to try fiction may seem like "lying"; to try dialogue may seem "voyeuristic"; to try autobiographical material may seem "self-indulgent" or like "betrayal." Yet one form is seldom adequate to any writer's lifetime work. First encouraging a writer to try a new form, and then, if that fails, offering to (just once!) change a paragraph of prose into a poem or a bit of autobiographical first-person narrative into third person for him or her sometimes breaks through the wall of seeming impossibility.

Jim Needs Confidentiality

Jim is a teacher in the public school system in my town. He is a favorite teacher of many young people. His classes in history are the hardest, most challenging, and most loved. It is common knowledge that students hold him in high esteem, remarking on how fair he is, how he does not play favorites, how he makes the First World War come to life in ways they can never forget.

Jim writes in my workshop for many months. He is working on a novel about a young man growing up gay in a strict, conservative religious environment. Sometimes, as he reads about the boy's family, how he was rejected and made to feel shame, he has to sit silently for a moment, waiting until he can resume reading.

Although we treat everything as fiction, it is clear to all of us that we hold knowledge about Jim that could cost him his job, cost him great suffering in this town. We will listen to his written work and respond with appreciation for his courage and integrity as well as for his exact images and psychological insight. When he brings in a manuscript, we will edit it carefully and give him back 12 copies with our comments on its strengths and its problems. In time, Jim will decide whether to publish his book under his own name or a pseudonym. But for now he doesn't have to worry about it. What he writes in the workshop will never be discussed outside the workshop.

> *Suggestion 12: Stress confidentiality.* All writers reveal themselves to some extent in their work, whether they intend to do so or not. Especially in reading our first drafts aloud, we allow others access to our secrets. This is a holy experience; this is revelation. It must be taken with the utmost seriousness and that which is revealed must be kept confidential.

THE WORKSHOP MEETING

We begin promptly at the announced hour. In my experience, if a group begins five minutes late two meetings in a row, almost everyone will arrive five minutes late to the third meeting. As leader, I respect those who have arrived on time by beginning on time. Latecomers learn quickly to arrive on time.

The First Writing Exercise

Members have been thinking about their writing on the way to the workshop. If we make announcements and do business first, that valuable, solitary centering can be lost. I don't want to waste it, and so I start with an exercise immediately after calling the workshop to attention.

My first exercise tonight is a collection of random objects. I place a cloth on the coffee table in the center of the circle, and bring a covered basket of objects to it. The objects are hidden from view because the element of surprise helps to jump start the imagination. I kneel with my basket beside the coffee table.

And then I say, "Now, if you already have in mind what you want to write, just ignore my exercise. I'm going to put out some objects. I want you to choose an object. Just choose something you'd like to hold in your hand. If you don't know why, that's good—it's best that way. Take the object with you to your chair, hold it in your hands, and see what memories or images come to mind. Then write anything that comes to you. Be free to stop and start; remember, you are making an artist's sketch."

I take my objects out of the basket. There are perhaps a 50 items, including a man's shaving brush, a seashell, an old whiskey bottle, a rusty horseshoe, an onion, a ball and jacks, a skate wheel, a baseball, a box of condoms, a crocheted doily. Someone starts to joke about the box of condoms. I stop her, saying that everyone is now searching for a memory, an association, so we must be silent.

People choose objects, and take them to favorite places in my house. Maria goes to the big chair in a corner of my study; Andy settles down at the far side of the kitchen table close to the brownies and the latest issue of the *American Poetry Review.* Amy takes a kitchen chair to the pantry and sits with her back to the door, near the cans of tomato sauce, the salt, the pepper, the jars of beans. Eva curls up in a corner of the big couch. George eases his back by lying belly down on the rug. Joan does not move from her place in the workshop room where she sits at the end of the sofa. Always.

We write together for 20 minutes. Then I call out to the group, "Can we please take just two more minutes to bring it to a place where you can go back to it later."

In two more minutes, I call out again, "If you need to go on writing, feel free to do that. Otherwise, let's gather here for reading." All but two of the workshop members gather in the room where we have first met. Two stay in other rooms, continuing to write. They may join us at any point in the reading time.

"Who would like to read first?" I ask.

Joan says, "Oh, I suppose I can, but this time it is *really* garbage!"

We laugh, because we all do this. We call it "apron wringing," as if we have wept into our apron so much it needs to be wrung out, or as if we are nervously twisting an apron between our hands.

Writers Who Apologize

When I first led workshops these apologies bothered me, and I tried to get people to stop prefacing their reading with put-downs of their own work. But gradually I have come to believe that even in the safest environment, reading our inner thoughts aloud is a vulnerable act, and discouraging people from expressing their anxiety can also be a subtle form of group censorship.

So, as time has gone by, I have rejoiced when writers are able to simply launch into their reading, *and* acknowledged that apologizing—apron wringing—serves an important function. Often an apology precedes a particularly vulnerable piece of work. We have come to anticipate that the larger the apology, the more important the work may be. Wringing one's apron seems to make the way safe; as if we ourselves want to the say the worst that anyone could possibly say, and then there is nothing to fear in what others might think. Observing each other apron wring has become a game in some of my workshops, with a comic touch of who can apologize most creatively.

Kathleen Moran, who has participated in my workshops for several years, began a "Collection of Classic Apron Wrings"—the "best" apologies given by members of our Thursday night workshop. She has divided them into five categories; some of those are as follows:

170

1. Apron Wringing That Is Pure Self-deprecation:
   "It's kind of messy, so you'll have to bear with me."
   "I think this may be an exercise in obscurity."
   "I enjoyed writing this, but I don't think you'll enjoy listening."
   "This is really, really awful."
2. Apron Wringing with Concern for the Group:
   "Okay, but you people are going to be really disappointed."
   "I didn't read this over, so you all are going to be in trouble."
   "After what I have heard here tonight, I shouldn't read, but since
       I spent my time writing, I guess I will."
   "I'm too intimidated tonight. You guys were great! Oh, all right."
3. The Sadistic Apron Wringer:
   "I suppose I should read this, because you people deserve to be
       punished."
   "So, you like trivial? I can give you trivial."
4. The Apron Wringer with a Sense of History:
   "I'll read while I have a voice, then I won't ever read again!"
   "The all-time great failure."
5. The Paradoxical Apron Wring:
   "I am not going to say my usual apron wring tonight, but..."

Our apologies are like a diver testing the board just before jumping, or an animal turning around and around before lying down. They are a way of preparing the way, preparing the place, reassuring ourselves, testing our voice before fully letting go. I do it myself—why not?

Reading Aloud What We Have Written

In this sharing time, the only work that is read aloud is work that has been written during the workshop writing time. This keeps all of us on an equal footing; we are taking equal risks; none of us has had the opportunity to revise. Also, it controls the amount of time each person takes; reading work that was written at home is much more difficult to keep within the bounds of available time.

171

Joan has chosen a strip of yellow plastic with the words "Police Line—Do Not Cross" printed on it in bold black letters. She is writing about a murder; it is part of a chapter in her mystery book. As she reads, we see in our minds the dark storeroom of a huge business building; we feel fear. When she has finished, I ask the group, "What did you like? What stays with you? What do you remember?"

Responding

A number of people speak briefly, mentioning the sense of danger, the image of the stacks of unused office furniture, the overwhelming sense of dark and silence. Joan nods, smiles, thanks us. Then another workshop member reads—a poem this time, very different in tone as well as in form. Again, we respond with what we like, and what we remember.

Peggy Gillespie asks each writer in her workshops to name one thing that he or she likes about his or her own work after others have responded. Her workshop members have found this a valuable way to strengthen their own confidence in their work.

Announcements and Manuscripts

Reading and responding to the work of all those who want to read, including myself, takes about an hour, which brings us to the midway point in the evening workshop. We have announcements of upcoming readings and our own news. Anyone who has received an acceptance or a rejection from a submitted manuscript can share it with the group.

If someone has brought a manuscript, he or she hands out a copy to each member for discussion the following week. I do not pressure people to bring in manuscripts. The only exception is when someone asks for pressure. For example, once or twice a year, Don Fisher asks me to "expect something" from him on a certain date. When that date arrives, I ask Don for the manuscript. For some people this is a great help; for others it creates instant writer's block!

If not many manuscripts come in, more time is given to writing in the workshop itself. A good balance between manuscript response and workshop writing needs to be kept. I have found that a gentle encouragement from the workshop leader results in the group helping to balance itself. On one evening we may respond to two manuscripts and write only once. On another evening there may be no manuscript and we may write twice or even have a third, short writing time.

I keep to our schedule faithfully, starting on time and ending on time; if there are 10 or 15 minutes left at the end of a session we may write for five minutes and share with no responses at all, rather than dismiss early. People who prefer to leave do so quietly, and the rest often have great fun in a very short writing exercise. At the end of Chapter Nine, I suggest some ideas for short writing times.

Problems with persons bringing in too much work, or wanting to read aloud typed work that they did not write in the workshop, can usually be solved by a private conference where the procedures of the workshop, and their reasons for being, are made clear.

Taking a Break

After announcements are made and manuscripts are handed out, we take a break for coffee, juice, brownies, carrot sticks, all of which have been available throughout the evening.

This is important time, because the writing and reading portions of the workshop are so structured there is little time for getting to know people beyond the written word. Usually we take 15 minutes for the break.

Manuscripts

After the break, we take out our copies of the manuscript that Michael gave us last week. It is five poems.

There are the writers who could bring in a wheelbarrow full of manuscripts weekly! Because these miraculous people do exist, it is a good idea to have some printed guidelines to give out at the beginning of every 10-week session. My guidelines say that people may bring in as much work as they want and hand it out to whomever they want. However, there are limits on what we can handle as a workshop. I myself will read not more than 20 pages of prose or five pages of poems per week. If a longer manuscript has been completed, the writer hands out copies and we take more than one week to prepare a response. The workshop will not discuss any one person's work two weeks in a row.

Michael's poems are dense and full of subtle innuendo. We talk long and deeply about two of the poems, telling him first what we like, what we think works well, and then telling him what troubles us. Two people disagree about one image: One person says it is unclear, the other says it is perfectly obvious. We do not try to decide between these two responses. We find out how many people agree that it is unclear, and how many people understand it. I tell the group that all the responses are "right," that is, all are honest responses by readers who do or do not understand the poem. What is helpful to the author is knowing how people respond. He will decide whether to change anything or not.

Everyone has written on his or her copy of the manuscript; I have encouraged them to write what they like as well as what troubles them. When we have finished discussing two of the poems, all the copies are returned to Michael with the letter I have written giving him my general response in addition to the specific comments I have made on the manuscript.

Giving and Receiving Help in Getting Work Published

Often I have a suggestion for publication possibilities, and we talk about it in the workshop. You can stay current on what literary journals and forthcoming anthologies are looking for by reading each issue of *Poets and Writers* and the *AWP Newsletter*. Keep a good current market reference or two available for your workshops.

At the end of each 10-week session, we have a potluck supper and Publication Party. All those who wish to do so bring multiple copies of manuscripts ready to send out, along with envelopes and stamps. I lay out on my coffee table stacks of sample journals, books of marketing resources, and a loose-leaf notebook of journal guidelines. Workshop members who prefer to write or are not ready to offer work for publication go into other rooms with an exercise I have prepared, and write during this time. Those who have already been published help those who have not; everyone shares knowledge and ideas.

One of the stories I love to tell at these parties was told to me by the novelist Jay Neugeboren. He insists that he had received 537 rejections before his first short story was accepted for publication, had received 1,000 rejections before his first novel, and had written eight novels before one was published! It is crucial for writers to understand that seeking publication is a process that will always involve more rejection notices than acceptance notices. A Publication Party helps because envelopes are addressed in an atmosphere of celebration and camaraderie.

A controversial word of advice: I encourage everyone to make multiple submissions unless they are sending to a journal that publishes monthly or to an editor with whom they already have a relationship. I myself am the publisher of a literary journal, *Peregrine*. I know the woes and problems of the editor. Nevertheless, it is unfair to ask writers to send work to only one journal at a time. Life is too short, and response is too slow. With few exceptions, literary journals cannot pay even if we accept work. As writers we must begin to value our own work and our own time. We must claim our own rights, with courtesy and sympathy for the problems of editors, of course.

The Second Writing Exercise

When everyone has settled down with writing pad and pen after the first exercise, I ask the group to remember a snapshot or a photograph of someone close, a family member or a close friend or lover. After a moment I ask them to start their writing with the words "In this one you are..."

People sit quietly for a moment, then some move to other places in the house—the big couch in the piano room, the chair in the study—and write. This time we have only 15 minutes to write, but by the end there are beautiful, moving pieces that are read aloud. We respond by saying what we like, what we remember. We encourage each other to go home, type the piece, work with it to revise, expand, cut, rethink it, and then bring it in manuscript form to the workshop where we can read it on the page and make our comments of appreciation and suggestions for change.

Closing the Workshop Session

We close at the preannounced time, 10:30. If some people have not yet read what they have written, I mention that it is closing time and allow those who must leave to do so. This eases the problem for those who have baby-sitters or other commitments, while making it possible for some of us to stay a little longer and allow everyone to finish reading.

As people prepare to leave, George and Connie stop at my chair to make an appointment for a private conference during the coming week. I encourage all of my workshop members to have at least one private conference with me during each 10-week session so we can talk at length about their writing. In that way I can become better acquainted with them and they can have an opportunity to tell me any concerns that they might not want to bring up in the group.

Eva is the last to leave. We talk for a moment in the doorway, and then we say goodnight. I will put the pages I wrote tonight into a drawer of my desk to wait until a day when I can rework it; Andy will leave his perhaps forever in his spiral notebook; Joan will stay up until the wee hours, typing, revising, preparing her manuscript to bring in to the group next week. Maria, I am sorry to say, will tear up the prose poem she wrote about a woman in a huge storm on the ocean clinging to a porthole looking into the churning water as her children sleep in their bunks. But she cannot completely destroy the vision that she created; I remember it.

ADDITIONAL EXERCISES

There are two kinds of writing exercises: those designed to get people started writing and those designed to improve craft. Until the emergence of the writing process movement, most books that included writing exercises were heavy on perfecting your craft and short on getting started. I am convinced that the best way to learn craft is to practice, to write, write, write (a variety of good exercises helps!), and, if possible, to have honest, sensitive, and thorough response from a supportive community of other writers.

Words begin to flow when the writer is no longer thinking about words themselves but rather seeing in his or her mind some concrete image. William Carlos Williams's decree "No ideas but in things" is basic to freedom in writing.

Writing exercises should stimulate the senses—all of them, not just sight—because that is how the world comes to us, and that is how we re-create what we have experienced or imagined. I have therefore included exercises in this chapter that involve sight, sound, taste, touch, and hearing.

The exercises described below are designed to trigger images, to get you started writing, and in some cases to assist specifically with some aspect of craft. In several exercises ("Making the Unfamiliar Familiar" and "Write about Writing," for example) I have suggested how having discussions following the exercises helps the workshop to consider matters of craft. The discussion can follow any of these exercises, as issues of craft arise within the members' written work.

These exercises are suggested for use in a workshop in which people are free to write in any genre (see Chapter Seven, which describes the workshop model), but all of these exercises can be used effectively by groups limited to only one genre, and almost all of them are also excellent for use by a writer working alone. In addition, the exercises in Part One, "Writing Alone," are also excellent when offered to a group.

GUIDELINES FOR GOOD EXERCISES

1. Make your exercises specific and concrete. Dick Bentley, a member of my Amherst workshop who recently completed his MFA in the Vermont College program, complained to me about exercises he had found in a book on writing. He said, "The exercises are too cosmic. The author tells you to write a 35-page story on God. I'd much rather describe God's hat." Dick's point is well taken. The best exercise is one that is clear, simple, and concrete. It triggers a memory, an association, an image. An onion pulled out of an ordinary paper bag and placed in a writer's hand will work magic; it may evoke dinners in a childhood home, weeding in a garden, walking through a farmer's market. Ironically, an onion with its layers and mystery may very well evoke a 35-page story on God!

2. Use surprise. Do not reveal your exercise until the moment of writing has come. Surprise is very helpful in triggering images.

3. Vary the mood of your exercises: serious, playful, outrageous. Let your own mood be your guide. The best exercise is the one that interests you at the moment you are offering it. We are all much more creatures of the atmosphere than most of us realize. Workshop groups arrive already subdued, noisy, tired, or funny. As you wait for the group to arrive, the only clue you have is how you yourself feel. If I am feeling quiet and want exercises that are inner and meditative, I frequently find the workshop arrives in a similar mood. Similarly, when I am feeling

178

excited and happy, often the door bursts open with people laughing and joking as they come in.

4. Always offer your exercise as an invitation, not a command. Give your exercise as a suggestion, inviting people to ignore the exercise if they already have something in mind to write. Even the best exercise can be a block if the writer is needing to write about something pressing at that moment.

5. Relax and trust the energy of the group itself to spark imagination. Something that surprises me but has become undeniable is the fact that images pass in silence from mind to mind in a workshop setting. Too frequently to be coincidence, several people will use the same image even though no one has mentioned it prior to the writing time. I first noticed this phenomenon one evening when three people wrote about an armadillo, and no armadillo had been mentioned. Since then, I have to come to realize that it goes on all the time.

Use a Good Exercise More Than Once

Ruth Bolton Brand, a writer who has been in my workshop for several years, has written obliquely and indirectly about the experience of her mother's suicide when Ruth was a young girl. I once gave as an exercise the guided imagery of standing in a doorway. Ruth had written in response to that exercise before, but for some reason this time she was ready to tell the story. She simply was a young girl at the closed door behind which was the bed her mother had left to go drown herself. I believe Ruth's story is brilliant: devastatingly clear, perfectly in the voice of a child. Don't hesitate to use a good exercise more than once.

After many years of leading workshops at the rate of three a week (four a week when I'm doing the volunteer workshop in a housing project)—I am still finding new ideas for workshop exercises. They are limitless, because the whole world is ours, exciting our senses, evoking our response, becoming our writing/art.

Seven-Minute Autobiography

Write a seven-minute autobiography in which at least one detail is fictional. At the end of seven minutes, the workshop members get three guesses for each piece of writing to determine what is fiction. This is an excellent opening exercise to use the first time people meet in a new workshop. I always tell the group that they must not worry about how well they write, that this exercise is just a game. After we have read and guessed (and usually laughed quite a bit) the workshop no longer feels like a roomful of strangers.

This opening exercise accomplishes several things: It warms the group up, gets everyone reading and responding, and demonstrates the fact that the group cannot tell whether stories are autobiography or fiction unless the writer volunteers the information. (See Suggestion 4, Chapter Eight. I recommend a discussion of this suggestion immediately following use of this exercise.)

The example below was written by Steven Riel, a young poet in my workshop in Amherst, whose first book of poems, *How to Dream*, is about growing up gay in a milltown in New England. Although the fiction is obvious, no one can know for sure whether other details are fictional or imagined. The cruelty of the schoolteacher is chilling and the writing effective, whether Steven lived or imagined the experience.

This time, I was born a girl. When, as a toddler, I watched my mother hang out the laundry in the backyard and exclaimed, "I'm going to have bras just like you when I grow up," this did not cause a single eyebrow to arch. My first-grade teacher still borrowed Marianne Skinner's purse to sling in the crook of her elbow while demonstrating to the class how I sashayed, but no one guffawed. The other girls studied her every movement, copied what they saw. When I paged with delight through the Sears catalog to assemble color-coordinated, mix-and-match outfits for myself, my parents congratulated themselves: they didn't have to worry about their Steven—possessed of such a blend of practicality and style, I'd go far.

Choose from a Group of Objects

When people are ready to write, put out a collection of objects that represent various kinds of experience: for example, a spool of thread with a needle stuck in it; an old, scarred wooden spoon; a man's shaving brush; a whiskey bottle; a horseshoe; a condom box; a small crystal ball; a dog whistle; a hand mirror; a baby rattle; a used baseball; a jump rope; and so on. I suggest you offer at least 30 or 40 small objects, as varied as possible. I have an old leather case that I found in a Salvation Army store; it holds all my workshop objects, ready to use again and again, and travels with me when I lead workshops in Ireland or Japan.

Each member of the workshop chooses an object, holds it in his or her hands, and allows it to trigger images from memory and imagination. This is the first exercise (after the warm-up Seven-Minute Autobiography) I offer to a new workshop group, because objects trigger each person's own story. Also, they suggest the world—how everything is full of metaphoric meaning, how everything can trigger our imagination.

In the writing example that follows, Deborah Campbell Softky, a writer in my workshop at the Graduate Theological Union in Berkeley, chose a key. This is what that key triggered for her:

In order to write, first you have to know that you exist.
Before I met my husband, I never knew what color my skin was. I didn't know that my skin was brown and smooth and shiny. I was BLACK. A social political concoction that I was dipped in. But I wasn't too black. No one ever called me Chocolate Drop. No one

paid me any mind until I was ten or eleven and some boy said, "She has a nice body but put a paper bag over her head." My best friend whispered this to me in my ear and I disappeared.

I never knew that I had breasts until my husband pointed them out to me. I mean, I knew that two things hung off my chest and they were big, and once, in junior high, when small breasts were in, I wanted to cut mine off. But I never knew that they were my breasts until I was 34 years old and I walked by a storefront window and there, sticking out through my blue Gap shirt, were these breasts! And they were nice ones, too. I went home and told my husband, "Look, I have breasts!" and he said, "I already told you that before. You're always forgetting."

I turned 35, and I discovered I had a body. A very nice body. It curved in at the waist and out at the hips. I found it early in the morning. The raging Furies weren't up yet. There it was in the full-length mirror. I went into the kitchen to tell my husband. I said, "Bill, I have a body," but he just looked at me and kept drinking his coffee.

My Old Testament teacher told me that I have a brain. He gave me a B-plus and I had never read the Bible before. I love him. He is like my father—getting bent out of shape over things, but he is also loving and compassionate, unlike my own father. I cry when I ask my teacher for a letter of recommendation for seminary. He puts his arm around me and says that everything will be all right. He has hairs growing out of his nose but I forgive him.

The black man is trying to drown me in the deep, dark sink. I slash at him with the jagged edges of a broken champagne glass. I escape down the driveway. It is covered with dead leaves. The phone is ringing in the bushes. It rings and rings and rings. I answer it. It is the police. "Help me, help me, I've been raped!" They won't answer me. "Okay." I say, "Will you come out if it's only aggravated assault?" The black man has buried a piece of glass in my knee. I wake up. I can't write if I don't exist. It's okay to

write if I'm not on the covers of magazines at newsstands everywhere. Does this end? No, it doesn't end. Not until the phone rings
and rings and rings, rings and rings and rings, and rings and the
voice on the other end answers and says, "May I help you?"

An interesting variation on this exercise was suggested to me by Margaret
Robison. She asks each person to choose five objects and arrange them in
an interesting relationship to one another, as if creating a kind of abstract
sculpture made of the objects. Then all members of the workshop look at
one another's arrangements and write whatever comes to mind.

Another variation I use frequently is to give all writers identical
objects. I have used onions, buttons, moth balls, cinnamon sticks, feathers,
screws (if I remember correctly, not *one* of the writers wrote about little
metal objects!), keys, dried grape tendrils, seeds, acorns, eggs, railroad
spikes, and so on.

EXERCISE 20:

Guided Imagery

Use guided imagery to suggest a remembered place. This is a powerful tool
for the workshop leader. Have people close their eyes (if they want to), and
for a few minutes lead the group in relaxation, suggesting that they be aware
of their own breathing, stretch out their feet and legs and let them be at
ease, then move on to the next part of the body, then the next, ending by
taking in a breath and letting it out, allowing all of the parts of the body to
come back together and be at ease. Then say, "Now travel back in your own
life to some time before this time, and find yourself in a doorway." (Instead
of a doorway you can suggest an old car, or in an upstairs hallway, a big chair,
a front porch, a swing, a secret place, looking into a mirror, waiting in line, a
workplace, in the dark, a city street, face-to-face with an animal, a schoolyard at recess, outside a closed door, or a bed, and so on.)

After you name the place, ask several questions to help the writers locate themselves there, giving them time after each question to silently find an answer. "What is the quality of light?" (If the place is a doorway, ask: "What is the quality of light in front of you? What is the quality of light behind you?" and "How tall are you in relation to the door handle?") "Is anyone near you, or are you alone?" Then say gently, "Stay there as long as you want. If something begins to happen, let it happen. When you are ready, very quietly pick up your pen and paper, and write whatever comes to you to write."

The first year I led my workshop in the Ursuline convent in Ireland, I used the doorway innocently, having no idea what a powerful image that would be for nuns, all of whom had entered the order when they were very young and before the huge changes of Vatican II had occurred. Every single one of them wrote about the doorway through which they left home knowing they could never return, even if a parent died, or the doorway through which they entered the convent. It was profoundly moving.

Sometimes this exercise will bring lyrical images to mind, sometimes funny images, and sometimes disturbing images, as in the following example by Christine Swasey, written in a workshop where I led a guided imagery and suggested they find themselves in a bedroom.

Night Feeding

In a dark room
where thin white curtains
bend and dance
in the evening breeze,
two beds stand side by side,
but only one child sleeps
under the eaves.
Beyond long windows
that face a pine-shrouded lake
the moon casts an arm of light
across tiny waves

184

softly touching against
a stone dock.
Alone in the house she sleeps.
The revelry at Auntie's next door
does not disturb
the rise and fall
of her small, flat chest.
Nor the cry of the lonesome loon
calling for his foraging mate.
Nor a fisherman in search of a catch
trolling his motor
past the stone dock.
Only the squeak
of the screen door below
and the sound
of heavy footsteps
on the stairs
open her eyes.
Awake now, she waits
to suckle the stick
thrust into her mouth,
and sip the sour semen
from its tip.

EXERCISE 21:

The Photograph Collection

Lay out a collection of photos and allow people to choose one or more as a trigger for their writing. An excellent source of photographs is secondhand photography books. Cut the pages from the spine with a razor blade or utility knife, and use the cover as a folder for the pictures.

Variations on this exercise include the following: Hold a container of black-and-white picture postcards over the writers' heads as they sit in a circle and have them pick one at random. Or, if the group has been together a long time, have them choose a photograph for the person sitting next to them.

Rebekah Boyd chose a postcard photograph of two people on a motorcycle leaping over a deep ditch. She wrote:

Lover's Leap

They hadn't really thought about it. They hadn't really calculated. They just hinged themselves together with her thin arms. Hinged themselves atop the sputtering motorbike.

"We can make it!" The heat swung from their torsos up into their faces while the bike spat, spat. He kicked a rock and she hinged her body, breasts flattened out against his back, hinged herself to his coat, grasping her fingers together just above his belt buckle. "We can make it, up and across!"

The snakes and small rabbits were gone, out of sight. And they hinged themselves. Excited.

The trees were points; reasons for stopping, for turning back.

"It's not that far," he shouted as they hinged and he twisted and revved and finally her feet came up and his feet came up and the bank across the mouth of the gully, the bank at the other side looked fluffed up with dead grass.

Their feet came up and they saw the dead grass while the trees were pointed but they didn't hear the echo, long and bellowing. They didn't hear the echo of the sputtering bike, the echo in the gully, in the opened jaw of earth before them. And they hinged and their feet came up and he turned to kiss her. He kissed her and twisted the black to rev and he kicked it to gear and they went. And they flew.

EXERCISE 22:

The Fragmentary Quote

Use a fragment of a poem, a sentence from a prose piece, or a few lines of dialogue from a play to trigger an image for your own writing.

In preparation for this exercise I often give my workshop members copies of several poems and prose pieces that begin with a quote that is used as an epigraph. The use of a short phrase or sentence as a trigger for writing, acknowledged in the text when appropriate, is a common and helpful practice among writers.

Sometimes the quotes I give are simply everyday things we say that may have caught my attention as people were speaking or in the middle of prose narrative: "You've done it again!" "If you promise you won't tell..." "I know I left it right here." "Don't touch that!" "You opened my letter!"

Sometimes they are lines of my own: "There is an argument in the trees tonight..." "The rain begins again..." "I am missing you..." "Death stands in the corner..." "A woman stands in the doorway..."

A young writer in my workshop in Berkeley told me that her writing group keeps a paper bag of quotes, and members reach into the grab bag for a quote to trigger their writing. My own workshops have created a shoebox full of what we call first lines of stories never written. It sits on a shelf in my library. Whenever someone feels in need of a little help, he or she dips into the box for a fresh idea.

Barbara Paparazzo wrote the prose poem that follows in response to the phrase "This is all you need to know." The end of the poem surprised me and moved me deeply, causing me to remember the dance, and the Obligatories, and to think about how life is a dance, and an Obligatory.

This is all you need to know. It is about Number 17. Number 17 is a difficult and beautiful Sacred Dance that was brought to the West early this century by a man named George Ivanivich Gurdjieff. The dance is done in a row of six people across, each performing his own movements in sequence to piano music. The dancers' feet beat the rhythm on the wooden floor. They wear white costumes with long waist sashes in yellow, orange, red, blue, green, and purple. There are 36 such Sacred Dances and 10 Obligatories. And this reminds me of Donald who had told me that AIDS is a gift that is allowing him to die consciously, savoring each moment, even if it brings pain. Pain is embraced as part of life.

I have used hundreds of quotes in workshops: phrases from works of fiction, single lines of dialogue from plays, lines or partial lines from poems. Some lines of my own, from poems in my book *Long Way Home,* are offered below as writing triggers. Every book on your shelf is rich with possibility. Each one alone can be offered as the stimulus for writing.

"Rain moves over the garden..."

"Your death is a hole in the universe..."

"I am a small man without a head..."

"I won't go back there this time..."

"We were young together..."

"Right before you disappear..."

"I told you when I left..."

"There was something that I asked of you..."

"Don't go. Don't stay..."

"She got quieter as she got old..."

"...the lake was still..."

"Here I cross a river..."

"...in a war that he does not believe in..."

"The soldiers explain..."

"...the sound of wild wolves howling..."

"I am still a long way from home..."

Write in Response to Music

Play music to trigger images for writing. I try to vary the music, both in style and in the generation it represents, so that different people are served on different evenings. When I play an oldie I try to choose something familiar even to young writers.

In the following example, playwright Tanyss Rhea Martula believes she wrote this scene in response to music that I played. I think she wrote it in response to a line about perfection in a poem of Jane Rohrer's, which I found in the *American Poetry Review*, January 1985. The fact that we can't be sure pleases me, because it illustrates the way the trigger works: It disappears once the imagination of the writer takes over.

I think I have never laughed harder than in the production of this scene, where the actor and actress were doing an exaggerated dance to increasingly florid music, while the woman talks and the man's expression becomes increasingly stoic.

ANNIVERSARY

Stage setting: a bare room except for a metal folding chair leaning against one wall.

A MAN and A WOMAN in their early 60's enter, dancing to the music "The Tennessee Waltz." The couple, dressed in their "anniversary" clothes, waltz around the room once or twice. The WOMAN begins to speak to her husband as they continue to dance, and as she speaks and her thoughts change and build, the music/dancing changes and builds, from waltz to tango to polka.

WOMAN (as they waltz)

You say this is perfect? This is in no way perfect, Henry. If you had any kind of memory, you'd know this wasn't perfect. In fact, this is the worst anniversary I've ever had. And, remember,

it's your anniversary too, Henry. Thirty-nine years of anniver-
saries and not one perfect one yet as far as I'm concerned. Do
you remember our very first one, Henry, our wedding day? Far
from perfect, wouldn't you say? Your gabardine suit was wrinkled, you forgot your spectacles so you couldn't even sign the
marriage certificate, Father Blinosky had to do it for you, and
you threw up all over me and Mama's wedding dress as soon as
we were in the car. Remember, Henry? I should've married
Charlie. I mean, then my memories would be different. They'd at
least have a chance of being perfect.

(The music slides into a tango.)

No, I haven't been keeping track of Charlie all these years,
but who knows, as smart as that guy was, he probably runs a
liquor store or at least a funeral parlor by now. And look at you,
Henry. Small repairs and lamp shades. I mean, who can make a
decent living on coffee grinders and lamp shade fringe?

(The tango gets wilder with lots of dipping
by the couple in the next section.)

And it's not that I don't forgive you for the throwin' up,
Henry. We all throw up every once in a while. Why, I even threw
up once, on our tenth anniversary, remember, Henry, when we
drove the Studebaker all the way down to Holyoke for the big
Bingo binge right before Lent, but you had to go that round-
about way and get lost? And I had my head in the map and got all
woozy and threw up all over the car 'cause I missed the ashtray?
Guess we were lucky to have the Studebaker, though Charlie
probably would've at least had an Oldsmobile or Pontiac by then.
Undertakers do all right, and liquor's always been sky-high.

(Music bursts into a polka as the couple
struggles to keep up.)

Perfect? No, I wouldn't say Charlie woulda made a perfect husband, I'm sure he woulda had his faults. As I recall, he used to pick at his fingernails in church. But, then, you used to do worse things than that in church, Henry, far worse than dirty fingernails. So don't talk to me about a perfect anniversary, or a perfect marriage or a perfect life or a perfect anything.

(They stumble and stop dancing, but the music continues. The WOMAN is upset.)

Just give me one perfect day, that's all I ask for. I've told that to Father Blinosky more than once. Just have God send me one perfect day and I'll be contented. One day when the septic doesn't back up...

(A phone rings offstage. The music stops.)

...one day when the kids don't call for money...

(The woman starts to exit as if to answer the phone.)

...one day when some dog doesn't shit on the lawn. Then, I'll say, yes, this is perfect.

(The WOMAN exits. The MAN is alone onstage. He starts to whistle very softly as he carefully takes out assorted pieces of a broken coffee grinder from the various pockets in his suit. He sits down and repairs the coffee grinder in a very slow but patient way as he talks to the audience...)

EXERCISE 24:

Write about a Sexual Experience

A first experience of sex or sexuality can be a vivid source of images for writing. First experiences of all sorts are fruitful; there is a list of suggestions in Lesléa Newman's excellent book of writing exercises, *Writing from the Heart.*

First sexual experiences are only the beginning of what is possible in writing about sexuality. The following piece was written in my Amherst workshop by actress-playwright Ruth Bolton Brand for a book she is writing about a grandmother's adventures with a man named Hank.

Sixty-Sex

He called and said, "I'd like to come and spend the night with you."

I didn't stop to think about how a feminist-oriented woman should react to this. I reacted as I reacted and said, "Oh—spend the night?"

"Yeah."

"Uh—sleep with me?"

"Yeah, I want to come and make love to you."

"Oh—well—uh—yeah—okay."

"Okay, see you in a bit."

"Where are you now?"

"In Boston—I'll be right out."

"Boston? Boston is 60 miles away."

"Yeah—at a pay phone—my time is almost up."

"Oh—okay, see you."

"See you later." End of phone call.

It's eleven at night. My cat and I retire early. We hardly ever have visitors. My little grandson comes down and we have make-believe tea. The granddaughters don't come. Hardly anyone comes. I lie still, thinking non-thoughts. Make love—make love—to Hank? My mind flips, my cat purrs. I still lie still. I won't get up and run around the apartment screaming for joy. This will upset my cat. She's very nervous. I pet her, thinking of how she broke the antique wedding plate when I got so hepped up over the married dentist coming to visit. That fiasco—what a fool I was. She knows it, my cat. She lies still, thinking everything's okay.

But I hop out of bed and start straightening up. I look in the mirror to examine the circles under my eyes. I go to the bathroom to wash, all the time thinking, Why should I wash? Make love? Make love with Hank? Oh my God, don't get worked up, keep cool, calm, collected. My cat is digging in her box trying to find a decent place to do her business—at least it's not on the rug. I will not be a doormat. I will not allow myself to be made a doormat of. I rub cream, then makeup under my eyes, I brush on mascara. No need for a diaphragm, no more of that. —I'll be dry. I haven't done it in so long. Shit, who cares. Well, I'll put a little cream down there. — He's going down there? Oh, my God. I'll put on a sexier nightie. —I don't have one. It's too cold for the long slinky sleeveless second, with the mended rip in the bottom, that I bought for the dentist and never wore. How silly! Kitty and I go back to bed and wait. I leave my old flannel gown on. To hell with it. Hank's only been here once before. Will he find the place at night?

After an hour or so I hear a loud radio, a car driving up beside my apartment window, the radio switching off. Suddenly silence. There's a knock. Oh my God—a knock on my door! Kitty braces herself. I rise from the bed, brace myself, and go to open the door. Hank is standing in the flesh, all six feet of him, bald in the doorway.

"Hi," I say.

"Hi," he says.

EXERCISE 25:

The Religious Image

Use images from your own religious tradition in a fresh way. These images are a rich source of metaphor. There is an example in Exercise 37 using Jewish imagery, and near the end of Chapter Four, using Moslem imagery.

In the example below, Teresa Pfeifer of my Chicopee workshop uses images of communion and of Moses in a natural, understated way to give depth and perspective to her poem about her son.

For My Son Robert: Novice, Age Five

You break bread into the center
of your large green net,
preparing your gift for the lake
as though a part of this communion
for centuries.

Pumpkinseed after pumpkinseed
finds its way to your offering. You
place each fish into your orange bucket
with the hands of a surgeon.
What a delicate operation!
You slip a large piece of bread
into the bucket.

The armies of children move in.
You defend these fish, insisting,
"Don't touch, don't hurt them."
Like Moses, you empty them back
by the parting of the waters.

My friend Maire O'Donohoe is a Roman Catholic sister who has written beautifully about the positive side of the life she has chosen in a convent in Ireland. In the poem that follows, she speaks with great courage about the pain that also attends that choice.

In this house I am alone.
In this house many women are alone—
together.
—Not open to the wonder of self,

the untried possibility, the flesh
behind roles.
And so, we shrivel
and whimper,
putter and expire,
and we do not touch—
for touch
opens sesames, and wild,
wild things tumble out
—unbidden—unbridleable—
and some can never be recalled.
And how can a nun dance with wildness?
and live
with memories of abandon?

Details of Direction

Write a piece in which you give a detailed description of a lesson, from the point of view of either the teacher or the learner. This is an excellent way to work on clarity of detail.

The following example is by Maria Black written on an all-day Saturday writing retreat in my home. As so often happens when a writer is faithful to detail, at the end this piece is about much more than the making of a dress.

Well, it wasn't a size 12½, but it was a Simplicity pattern, a dress, and it had darts. We were in the guest house, down the hill from the Big House with its shaded porch, and my sisters were down by the river. We could hear their voices. It was summer, hot as hell, but there was a breeze coming through the screens. The grasshoppers (was it grasshoppers?) made a loud background noise that will forever remind me of summer and my childhood.

It was my first sewing project. The thick blue cotton was spread out on the floor, smoothed by my own small tanned hands neatly against the straw rug. It was a thick, substantial cotton. It would make a durable dress. It would have buttons down the front and a scooped neck. The white large flat buttons were in a small brown bag from Calico Corners we'd brought from Houston, my mother and I, to Hunt. And today she'd teach me how.

I pinned the delicate onionskin paper to the material, my mother showing me how to line up the arrows with the grain of the fabric, the weave of the fabric. She held it while I wrestled with the pins, awkwardly. She was always a good teacher, patient, encouraging, letting me struggle. When the pieces were all pinned, she pulled out her scissors, the special ones, pinking shears, and I held the heavy things along the line of material marching up, sawing up, chewing cleanly up and down the lines of my blue dress, around the curves where my neck would be, my arms, all the while my young mother, younger than I am now, watching me, well aware of the occasion, marking my face, smiling I'm sure to see the rapt concentration.

I especially remember the feel of finally turning over the clipped and notched facing around the neckline, pinching the seam with my fingers, smoothing the thick blue, as solid and substantial as any summer day could be, as normal and routine as any mother's love, folding it over and watching my mother show me how to whip it down. Her fingers moved so surely, the needle's tip so close to them. She didn't use a thimble, said it got in her way, but she gave it to me to wear when I took over. It was a silver thimble, Lallie's, her mother's, already dead, dead and cold and gone forever: that mother.

I remember the hot dry grass of the hill leading down to the Guadalupe, the shady bank and the scrub oaks, their roots exposed and white with the wear of little feet. I remember the swing, held back on a nail until used, then standing up high on that tree's roots, higher than the others with the stick of the swing held out before me, in front of my new pale skin, and my conversation with myself before I pushed off, a conversation alone inside my head yet self-conscious as if the world was watching, then no thoughts but the body deciding when to let go.

EXERCISE 27:

Making the Unfamiliar Familiar

Describe a scene you know very well, which others may not know. This may be an intimate scene, such as shaving in the bathroom, getting undressed in the high-school locker room, or observing a place where you have lived—a house, a main street.

I have used a variation of this exercise to demonstrate the value of writing about what we know. It worked particularly well when a new woman joined my workshop who had lived for many years in China as the wife of a member of the United States Foreign Service. No one in the workshop knew this fact but me. Without any previous announcement to the woman, Sherry, I asked the workshop members to write for just five minutes a description of a street market in China. I had all of us all read our descriptions (I wrote one as well) and when we were finished, I asked which of us had really been to China. There was no doubt. Everyone in the room had written awkward, stereotyped images of naked chickens hanging upside down and lacquered dishes like we had seen in Chinatowns in the United States. Only Sherry's description was rich, colorful, and surprising, full of Chinese words, images, scents, sounds of a street market. Then we talked about the fact that each of us comes from a place of intricate, interesting detail, if we will just write it so others can see, taste, smell, touch it.

The example that follows was written in a workshop by Sharleen Kapp.

It is about a place where she lived for several years:

The Subject Is Flies

The subject is flies, and dry dust blowing across the crusted earth—its surface cracking open like a large yawning mouth hungry for moisture.

The subject is babies with stomachs swollen—mud caked, crouching down to poke at the bursting, baking lizard—it, too, packed in mud.

The subject is leather thongs, and spear throwers, and billibongs, and brown skins and black, pink freckles, deep browed foreheads and loneliness.

The subject is Dreamtime, the source of all understanding; a direct connection to God (pale skinned flying man), a Dreamtime journey with the hammer thrower.

They gather together before the rainy season and create strange music, throaty lingering passages that travel down seven foot long horns, carved wooden instrument—treasured—sacred, passed from father to son.

The men gather in the evening to share rude jokes and join in the games, the rabbit kill.

The women, blond curls or black, thin breasts loose, long sinewy muscles, balance the youngest child on one hip, standing by the one hut, outback trading post.

Dusty children, boys and girls, dancing around the edges, chewing loudly on wichity grubs, happy. They take their places at the fire waiting for the lizard to burst, hot and juicy out of its mud blanket.

The men rest their instruments and talk slowly, gutturally. The subject is flies.

EXERCISE 28:

Taste Buds

Offer bite-size pieces of something to eat and see what this food for thought stimulates. I have used thin slices of lemon, half slices of homemade bread, ripe cherries, strawberries, and slices of raw carrot, raw potato, and apple.

In a workshop held in my home, Martha Ayres wrote in response to a raw potato:

The First Potato

Papaw scooted, his legs leading
along the cool rich earth
past the row of corn to the potato patch.

I scooted with him.

Papaw's legs,
as far back as I could remember,
were all twisted from arthritis.

That never stopped him planting
the most beautiful garden
in the world.

He planted.
I covered.

I covered each little seed
with the exact amount of dirt
except for the potatoes.

Potatoes have eyes.

Papaw placed the eyes in the ground

and covered them very gently.

This moment seemed to me
as solemn
as eating the wafer
and drinking the wine in church.

Papaw was my best friend.
I could look right into his eyes.

He carried a wonderful pearl handled pocket knife.
Sometimes, he even let me carry it
to the garden.

In August, there would come that day
when Papaw would look out over the garden,
see the green leaves of the potatoes,
nod to me, and off we'd scoot.

He'd stick his gnarled hand into the black earth
and pluck out a big beautiful potato,
dust the dirt off on his pant leg and clean
it a little more on his shirt tail.

Hurry Papaw, hurry.

He'd take out the pearl handled knife,
pull the silver blade from the handle,
slice off a piece of potato
and hand it to me.
I loved the first potato,

the taste of earth still clinging to each slice.
He'd slice another piece for himself,
one for me,
one for him,
one for me,

until it was finished.

Papaw would close the knife,
put it in his pocket, lean back
and look at the sky.

I would do exactly what he did,
lean back and watch the clouds drift by.

In that silence
nothing else mattered.

Just Papaw,
the pearl handled knife,
the potatoes and
me...

EXERCISE 29:

Questionnaire

Have the group call out answers to several questions about each of two
characters, then everyone writes using some or all of the answers. Peggy
Gillespie used this exercise recently in a workshop at the Hampshire County
House of Correction. Some of the questions she asked and the answers
given by the writers are listed below:

Character's name?	Tom-Tom	Amanda S.
Place of residence?	Albuquerque	Maine
Pet?	piranha	cat
Favorite item of clothing?	cardigan	spandex
Strangest item of clothing?	elevator shoes	fake fur
Hates?	electric can openers	false teeth
Favorite food?	pork fried rice	Oreos

Religion?	Hindu	Jehovah's Witness
Collects?	old cars	beer can tops

This exercise is fun for a group and is especially good for evoking humorous writing. Almost always there is surprise and laughter as people share the many different ways a single image has been used. And often a writer goes on to develop a piece into a successful short story.

In response to Peggy's exercise, James Gryszan wrote an imaginative, jazzy piece.

It was an acrid and hot day. A dust storm was developing out in the suburbs of the New Mexican town of Albuquerque. Tom-Tom had to interrupt Jack's game to feed the piranha school. The tank was aburst with clicking, hungry man eaters. Tom-Tom said he was a Hindu. No meat for him. But to stay in touch with the compromises of reality's many swinging doors, he enjoyed the devouring of meat flesh substitutes.

He had an idea. He would get dressed and go to the Hippy Shoppe Cafe and read some poetry. Get dressed in his cardigan sweater and elevator shoes and obsessively clean machine, his 1952 Sunbeam-Air amphibian vehicle. Out here in the desert it doesn't rust, he said. Yes-sir-ree. There he was stemming a proud stance and a glint of amusement in his eye. He arrived downtown.

First thing through the door. All the Mothers of any kind of invention were all gathered in one. He was on top of the list. He sat down at a table, ordered from the waitress pork fried rice and a copy of Along the Watchtower by Jehovah. The head hip hop in this place. The Branch Davidians were doing their set poetry reading and then Tom-Tom could sign.

Just then he spotted on the rug beside him a group of girls all dressed in black; top to toe was spandex riddled with holes. She was eating Oreos, and as she smiled she spoke. "Hi, my name is Amanda S."

"Pleased to meet you Ms. Where you from?"

"Well I'm down from Maine. I saved beer can tops which sponsored my Fish Out of Water Poetry Series."

Dream Image

Images from dreams are already works of art, metaphors for meanings we ourselves often only dimly understand. Begin with an image from a dream and write freely, letting words and associations come as they will, without imposing any necessity of order.

Kazue Yano, in my workshop in Japan, wrote the following poem using a dream image.

To an Unborn Child

I have never dreamed of you
except in my dreams.

So many unspoken words ring
like noisy bells in my silence:
"Sorry, I have no intention to marry."
"I have to finish college."
"I've got to get myself a job."
"I want to go to grad school."
"I need a career."
"Oh, I hate my husband."

After all these years of
bleeding in vain,
you appeared in a dream one night.
I am not sorry and I won't be

sorry for not seeing you in person.
But you may stay in my dreams as a
guardian angel,
if you want to.

The Sense of Touch

Write in response to something that has a characteristic texture. I have used cotton balls, sandpaper, modeling clay, pieces of silk cloth, samples of braille, chestnut burrs, cockleburs, smooth stones. Have writers close their eyes, then place the object in their hands. Before they begin to write, ask them to allow themselves to experience the sense of touch without looking.

I have heard of writing groups that put people in pairs and have them close their eyes and touch one another's hands or face, then write a description of the other person. I myself have not used this exercise. I think this kind of thing should not be attempted unless a group agrees to try it. Keeping your group safe, keeping boundaries clear, is the workshop leader's responsibility. Perhaps the reason I have not tried it in my workshops is my own sense that it would not be comfortable for me.

Below, Florence Keene writes in response to having a piece of sandpaper placed in her hand.

Two sides, one rough, one smooth. *Like life,* I think as I feel it, and it's wonderful how balanced I feel just holding this in my hands.

I tend to think of my life as having more of the rough than smooth and I think I've forgotten so many good things that have happened to me like I suppose the time Momma let me climb up on her lap and read to me. I can still see it, feel it. She was sitting in the maroon chair over in the corner of our living room engrossed in the nightly paper. It was a Thursday night and the food specials were being advertised for Friday's sales. Her voice was husky and strong as she started reading aloud, "Bananas two pounds for 10 cents; apples three pounds for 12 cents; DUZ soap powder, one large box 25 cents," and she didn't notice that I had crept up on her lap and snuggled myself in against her soft bosom. I was so happy and so thrilled, I was afraid to breathe for Momma told me repeatedly those days that I was too big to sit on anyone's lap anymore, especially Grandma's whose lap I was constantly in.

Momma kept reading off the items as I lay there contentedly and secure, reveling in my good fortune. Her voice droned on and on until, suddenly noticed, I was pushed off her lap onto the floor. I knew even then—I was five—that my age wasn't the problem. Momma wasn't a demonstrative woman, but I tucked that experience away and it has warmed me all my life. It was the only time Momma ever read to me.

EXERCISE 32:

"I/You"

Write addressing another person, unnamed, as "you." The "you" can be yourself or someone else, an animal, or an inanimate object. After the writing, it is a good time to discuss how writing to someone or to something helps focus the work by making the audience clear. Suggest the possibility of changing to third person or first person in final draft, if desired.

The example that follows was written in workshop by Donald Fisher.

A Poem about Love and Astronomy

I see you
through panes of glass.
I can't touch you
but I do wave.

You wave back
dip your head at me
smile.
The smile shows I think
that you really mean it
you really are happy to see me.

Encouraged
I decide on a gift for you.
What could be better than a star?

So I reach up and clutch one
pull it down
it doesn't burn my hand.

I present it to you wrapped
in brown paper.
You're pleased of course.

As brown paper opens
like a flower in the morning
the star glows
burning a small black hole in your table.

My cheeks flush red
and I wonder why
I can't do these things right.

EXERCISE 33:

The Fearful Scene

Write a scene in which you felt fear. Make the details so clear, so concrete,
your reader will feel the same fear. In the following example, Dee DeGeiso

wrote a memory that she had "carried around in her head for 32 years." Dee is a playwright who helps all of us in the workshop think about good dialogue. This piece is a powerful beginning of what will become a short story.

Everyone got quiet when the boy walked down the street. He was about 14 years old, wore a Brooklyn Dodgers baseball jacket and carried a navy blue briefcase. He was black, a colored boy, probably from down below 18th Avenue.

"What's that coon doing here?"

It was a hot August night, sunset. A gang of kids of all ages was hanging out on the Casale's porch. the older boys were smoking cigarettes, the younger ones were sucking Popsicles. Darlene and Rae-Anne sat on the top step polishing their nails.

"Hey, jungle-bunny, where d'ya think you're going?"

The boy stiffened slightly but kept his gaze straight ahead. He increased his pace but didn't run.

"Hey boy, didn't you hear me? Where the hell d'ya think you're going? Wise-guy nigger. Aren't you gonna answer?"

"Let's go after him."

Billy, Swaf, and Johnny T. stubbed out their cigarettes and slowly moved toward the boy.

"Leave him alone. He's probably just cutting through."

"Pipe down, Rae-Rae. You want him messing around your house when you're sleeping?

"Maybe he's lost."

"Well, we'll just help him find his way, won't we?"

"Need a little push, boy?"

The boy started to run then, slipped slightly, then regained his balance and took off at full speed toward the brook at the end of the street.

"Let's get him."

The younger kids cheered as Billy, Swaf, and Johnny T. began the chase.

"What are they gonna do to him? Billy has a knife."

"Yeah. And brass knuckles too."

"He didn't look dangerous to me."

"Yeah. Well, I guess we can't have them coming around here."

Rae-Anne and Darlene looked down the street but the boys were out of sight. Mr. G. called out from his upstairs window, "I hope they get him. We don't need no niggers around here. They'll teach him a lesson. You girls oughta go inside. It's getting late." And he was gone.

"Rae-Anne, let's go down there."

"I'm not going anywhere."

"He may need help."

"Are you crazy?"

"They could kill him."

"They'll just beat him up. They'll kill us if we show up. I'm going in. Wanna come?"

"No. I'm gonna let my nails dry first."

The younger kids had drifted across the street and Darlene was alone on the porch. She wondered what was in the boy's brief-case. A composition pad. A pencil box. A large soap eraser. Maybe some ballpoint pens. He liked the Dodgers. Her father said the Dodgers were bums. What did his father say? She had been taught to stay away from the colored, but was never given a reason. Her mother told her never to look at them, to encourage them. They lived in dirty houses on dirty streets, drank too much and didn't work. Except for some of the women who were maids for the rich Jews on Mount Vernon Place. Why did he have to come here? He must have been scared. Did he think he could just sneak by? What were they doing to him? Darlene had been Billy's victim since she was five. Swaf's too. They had thrown lit matches at her feet, pushed her face into the snow, bumped her too hard when she was roller-skating. And she was white. And a girl. What were they doing to him?

She decided to go down to the brook. It was almost completely dark. She had never gone down to the brook in the dark.

The Absolute Relative

Write about a family member—one of those stories that is repeated when
the tribe gathers. Every family has legends, tales of adventure, humor, or
horror. It is a rich source for the short-story writer. Cynthia Kennison has
received prestigious prizes and awards for her short stories and her plays.
This is one of her family stories, which she swears is true:

A Fatal Attraction

Mosquitoes will hate this smell. We light the citronella candles on
the picnic table, and mosquitoes will fly away and break their
stingers on the black birch trees and fall onto the floor of the forest. The candles smell good to us. Really. Comforting, like something you rub onto pulled muscles. Only you don't have to put any
onto yourself, and that is very important.

My Uncle Randall still attracts moths in the summer. They fly
out of the evening air, indoors or outdoors, into his hair, his ears,
up his sleeves, his shorts. Sometimes in the afternoon, when he
carries the *New York Times* from his cottage to my father's,
when the odor of the hemlock needles he walks on rises and sur-
rounds him like Christmas, my uncle arrives with a white moth or
two clapping slowly on his white crew cut.

It was in the *New York Times* he read about eradicating
gypsy moths in a way that wouldn't hurt the environment. The
idea was to keep them from mating with each other, to decrease
their numbers through birth control. My uncle wants to do the
most harmless thing, always.

My aunt and uncle came up from New Jersey for the summer with a crate of little golden plastic cages that looked like lanterns. They were sex traps. Uncle Randall assembled these traps before he hung them in the branches of the hemlocks, the spindly oaks, the white birches whose silver leaves trembled like moths flocking. He had to place in each trap a receptacle of a potent potion. The potion's job was to mislead every male Gypsy moth in the forest to believe he would mate with a trap. Instead, of course, he used up his sexual energy, and that was that in the procreation game for him.

My uncle, on a short wooden ladder, hung his sex traps and climbed down and waited. The first swarms of moths beat themselves to death—or ecstasy, we couldn't tell—in the traps. My uncle rubbed his hands with glee and thumbed his nose while my father compulsively wrapped tree trunks with electrician's tape and watched caterpillars climb to the cottage eaves. The moths loved my uncle's potion.

The moths also loved my uncle. They still love him. The instructions on the trap crate said you mustn't touch the sex potion. Even a tiny drop on your skin, anywhere on you, will be absorbed into your own chemistry, your soul maybe, and never leave. You will forever attract moths. Not only gypsy moths; they are gone now. But other kinds.

"You won't need to mark my grave," Uncle Randall tells my aunt. "Save the money. Just look for moths diving for my spot in the earth."

EXERCISE 35:

Face to Face with an Animal

Close your eyes and imagine yourself face to face with an animal. Then write what you saw in your inner eye.

210

Brooke Sullivan wrote the following poem in response to this exercise:

God watches as each sparrow falls
and they do, myriads of them,
from the cold; frozen;
clenched in a cat's jaw,
flickering, fighting to stay alive.
They are in the abandoned barn,
above the cornice down the street.

This fall as all color left the fields
the leaves fell, sumac standing
like soldiers along the ridges
guarding the slope up from the river.
Little birds: chickadees, tanagers,
lit on the sumac, raced
around the wounded oak torn by lightning
in the tangled yard of the abandoned barn.

What I mean to say is that
there is no stopping the fall.
Swift and sad
and a prickly cold over the legs and arms
as birds are discovered,
fallen, gray tufts of down
matted in the cracked bones
washed up with the wooden debris
littering the river bank.
And in the fields, ridged
and plowed away for winter, the dog
hunts in the mud clumps for remains
of birds.

EXERCISE 36:

Magical Realist

Write without making "sense" in the usual way. This is a wonderful exercise for springing the imagination out of its usual tracks. Invite workshop members to allow impossible things to happen in the midst of realistic narration. Suggest using disconnected sentences, disconnected images for five minutes, then use that material as a trigger for further writing. This is easier for some people than for others.

The following example is a prose poem written in workshop by Dan Nissenbaum.

> There is some soil in my soul now; I found it there today. Around about the 16th night, a tomato came up. I stared at it until it grew dark, and then my father pulled me away. His hand touched my shoulder lightly. "All right," he said, "it's all right."
>
> Nobody could find me. I was living in a little cavern by myself, me and a few pictures on the wall, a few little pieces of food, a desk, a chair, a desk, a chair, a chair, a chair. Lantern on. Nine hundred light bulbs next to them, and an ax on a stand. Question was, stuck here, would I ever take the ax and smash through the light bulbs?
>
> Stuck, picking through the pieces in the dark, feeling the filaments on the floor, cutting my hands and feet and toes on little shards of glass, and wondering if someone would come and get me. I kept thinking, "they never did, they never did," only every time I said it I figured, "maybe she will, maybe she will."

Another good way to assist writers in breaking habitual patterns of writing is the Random Word exercise suggested in Chapter Six. The exercises "Surprise Yourself" in Chapter Five and "The Scrambled Egg Poem" in Chapter Six are also valuable in helping writers in workshops discover new ways to approach their writing.

EXERCISE 37:

A Special Day

Write using images of a holiday or special occasion. Family gatherings are rich with intense emotion and memory. Begin with an image of a holiday, a birthday, a wedding, a family reunion, or some other special day.

Elana Klugman wrote this poem on an evening when she chose to attend workshop rather than stay home for Yom Kippur.

Yom Kippur

When the *shofar* blew this year,
I was not in the Land.
I was underground, in a place
where the sound couldn't reach me. I was
washing that roasting pan
that had sat for seven
days and seven nights.
I was rinsing diaper after diaper,
not the cleansing
that the *Neilah* sings of.
When the *shofar* was blown
I was sorting out between the needs
of two hungry children,
cutting cheese, beating eggs with a baby
at my breast. As the Book of Life
was shutting on the year to come
I was cleaning the refrigerator
so the door would shut
and hold the rotting food
there had been no time to clean out.

Am I in Jerusalem this year or outside

the wall? Feasting or fasting?
This year I was on the other side
of the *mehitzah*
where the sounds of children
are louder than prayer.
This year I was the *shofar,*
the wail and the summons.

*Note: "Neilah" is the closing prayer for Yom Kippur. "Mehitzah" is a barrier
used in Orthodox Jewish synagogues to separate men and women.*

EXERCISE 38:

Write about Writing

Suggest that everyone write how they feel about their writing, about the
workshop itself, or about concerns that have come up in relation to their
work. Once in a while it is a good idea to give a group the opportunity to
reflect out loud together on what is happening within the individuals in their
group. This exercise is a good way to stimulate discussion and include those
persons who tend to be shy about sharing their questions or problems.

Below, Sarah Browning raises a very difficult question for writers. After
she read her piece aloud, the workshop responded with an excellent discussion about personal and political writing. When this happens, it is good to
relinquish your planned agenda and allow the group to take its time in exam-
ining a question of craft or conscience. To assist our discussion on this occasion, I introduced Carolyn Forché's poem "The Colonel," which is overtly
political, and Grace Paley's two-and-a-half-page story "A Man Told Me the
Story of His Life," which is subtly political. Here is Sarah's piece:

Maybe this exercise will work for me another time. Sometimes
when I'm distracted and I force myself to focus on the exercise I

214

do come through the other side to an interesting piece of writing. But tonight I'm cluttered. I'm not receptive.

Then I came home and read the *Boston Globe* and talked about the defense budget with Tom. I'm making arguments in my head about the possibility of further cuts in the military.

I wonder how possible it is to write about that kind of rage. Sometimes my rage at injustice in the world absolutely consumes me. I am physically torn to pieces. I can't even now seem to say what happens to me when I think of women living on welfare checks of $375 a month.

Why is it simple to write about suffering on a personal level— or rather about the pain one has experienced from others—but not about the pain one experiences at knowing about systemic injustice? It is that the pain people inflict on each other is always complicated? That there are ambiguities? Is it that only writing about specific, personal experiences, even if they are not one's own, is the kind that "works"?

EXERCISE 39:

A Series of Words or Images

Poet Carol Edelstein, who has led workshops using the AWA model, told me about this exercise, which came to her from another writer. She uses it frequently in her workshops, because it gives everyone several triggers for starting a new work and seems to break the natural shyness many people have about beginning to write in a group setting.

Call out one ordinary noun (*flea, tree, apple, mother, mirror,* and so on). Everyone writes for 30 seconds. Call out another noun, and everyone writes for another 30 seconds. Do this several times, then give the group 20 minutes or more to write anything they choose to write.

A variation on this exercise is the following: Give the writers a collection of images to write from, calling them out at intervals described above or three at a time for a full writing period: a cracked mirror, winter ice, a light bulb; or a lollipop, a dirty comb, a fishhook; or a wildflower, a sidewalk, a doorknob. Workshop members are free to use only one, two, or all three in their writing.

A good variation is to ask the workshop to provide images. I give people three minutes, ask them to list at least 10 images, then have individuals call the images out at random, inviting others to write down any that are of interest. People then choose one or more images and write.

It was the image of broken glass that triggered the piece below by Jim Eagan:

> Seth stabbed the floor with his cane, trying to maintain balance on his wobbly old shanks. He careened across the room toward the third-story plate-glass window, unable to slow his momentum. There was a deafening crash as he hit the glass with his cane-side shoulder. He was airborne, dropping at an ever-increasing speed.
>
> He opened his eyes and closed them immediately. In that moment he glimpsed the shattered glass suspended like crystals in the air all around him. He saw the street coming up to meet him. When he closed his eyes he saw his father standing before him, arms outstretched, with a glow of light around him. In the light that surrounded his father, Seth saw shadows of other people; they seemed familiar in some way, although he couldn't see them clearly.
>
> "No, no," a loud voice shouted in his head, "I can fly. Don't you know I can fly?" He tightened the muscles all over his back and began to breathe deeply. Flinging his cane away, he raised his arms like giant wings that caught the evening sun and shot a crystal-clear blast of white light into the eyes of the people in the street below.
>
> They covered their eyes for a moment, and when they looked again the street was strewn with shattered glass. An old

man's broken cane lay against the curbstone, and three magnificent, silver-tipped feathers drifted softly to the ground.

EXERCISE 40:

From the Mundane to the Marvelous

Read a nursery rhyme, a recipe, a schoolyard chant, or a set of directions from one place to another, an advertisement, or a provocative want ad or item from the personals column or police report in the newspaper, to get the writing started.

In my Chicopee workshop, one of the writers, Enid Santiago Welch, has begun two workshops—one for her neighbors and one for children in the housing project. She clipped provocative words and phrases from newspapers and glued them to three-by-five cards and passed them around for her writers to use as triggers. It worked beautifully!

In my workshop at the Graduate Theological Union in Berkeley, a young writer named Ali Hall opened my eyes to the possibilities of the recipe when she wrote the following prose poem, which she titled *"Here"*:

Here. This is how you do it. Once you've measured out the cup and a half of flour, the white unbleached kind heaped up fluffy in the scooper and leveled off gently with a flat edge, you sprinkle around some sea salt and baking powder until you can't exactly find it anymore. You can set this aside for a long time. The butter you begged to soften quickly because you didn't take it out in time now gets to be sliced up with other great stuff like cream cheese. It's a secret, one that *rugelach* and *hamentaschen* bakers know, that cream cheese is magic, making things smooth and slightly not too sweet, that special something that makes your guests pull you aside in the kitchen, if they're really noticing. You put it all together, and when you get your dough the way you want

217

it, then it can sit too. That's when you get to think about the berries. It's best if you have two kinds, sometimes more. But you never use strawberries because they get swollen and mushy and dead tasting. Blackberries, the Marion kind, and boysenberries, loganberries, and raspberries are a good combination when they make a balanced, deep dusky purple palette and their little berry membranes give up nectar, popcornlike, at just about the same time. And if you pick the raspberries yourself, try and get there when God does, just before the birds and the sun, when the berry kernels' hair stands out and the skins are strong enough to hold as many dewdrops as your tenderly grasping fingers. Also, take enough to freeze for later. When you mix some sugar with your berries, check and see if they are as sweet as yesterday's, listen as you taste, one-two-three, and if the sweet has pleased its way off your tongue, they're probably just about right. Remember, you've got the cream cheese trick on your side. And sometimes when you scrape it all into a pan you like for bubbling and bursting the berries around the golden pads of dough, its got the tum-tump-tumping of a Bach oboe concerto. But only sometimes.

EXERCISE 41:

Stream of Consciousness

Write, as fast as you can, everything that comes to your mind. A therapist in my workshop once informed me that each of us has 70,000 thoughts a day. What a steady stream of material for writing!

Jennifer Bryan, a psychologist, wrote this moving response to her work life. The absence of periods and the breathless pace does a brilliant job of communicating the intensity of the experience as well as the sense of an ocean of human need in which the doctor is working.

Rape, she's 15 I didn't ask about her ethnicity or culture she's so different from me yet I know her I know her see her did she wear that orange lipstick for me, is her hair always so neat and clothes so clean or did she fuss over herself for me for coming to the doctor for talking about the dirty rape the horrible touching and tearing and lies he told, did she bring a 10-year-old friend because she knew how white I'd be, how tall, how rich-looking and smart-sounding, how my heels would click click on the hospital tile as we walked to my office, the 10-year-old who she's looking after who she wanted to have wait when her own sister wouldn't, when her grandmother wouldn't come at all, and my needing a signature on the forms and my needing the insurance card and grandmother's got no phone and Ladeeta's just 15 and the man was 45 and she cried when she told me but I didn't start there because I knew how it would hurt and so she told me other things about her father dying and it was five years ago and she went to live with her grandmother because her father said that would be best, Ladeeta said my mother do drugs and he didn't trust her, but grandmother was good and she took care of Ladeeta and her father both because the father got sick and stayed at home and went to the hospital and stayed at home and went to the hospital and stayed in the hospital and died at home because he got the sickness and I said the word, not like a question—AIDS—and she nodded and the tears were there before we even got to the man to the neighbor who said he was taking her and Treneese to eat out but he lied and it was a bar in Chicopee and Ladeeta said we was minors; I knew not be at no such place, and I've got a history to gather a thorough history presenting problem psychosocial family school medical previous psych contacts suicidal homicidal Axis I Axis II Axis III Axis IV Axis V, she was 30 minutes late, I'd almost gone home and then she was there and the 20-year-old sister who didn't want to stay and the 10-year-old friend and no grandmother to sign the papers and the secretary asked me do you still want to see her and I said yes even though a place inside had called out no, no I do not want to hear this story, I do not want to sit across from dark Ladeeta who is so beautiful and too grown up and awkward and graceful both, I don't want to hear how he drove to the woods and locked all the doors and told her she'd like it and told her she'd be feeling good, like a woman and I want to lift up my pen right here and stop the writing of this story and stop the telling and stop the feeling of fire and sickness in my gut that no pen can douse no telling can fully cure no sleeping will erase because Ladeeta is 15 and he hurt her and he gave her diseases more than one and maybe the one that killed her father I can say the name, I can say it—AIDS—and Ladeeta, she can't read, she told me that, she can't read, had such a hard time in school always something taking her mind from the books or the sound of the teachers voice and she doesn't want to go back to the grandmother's house where she's lived since her father died in 1987, she lives with her sister, the one who didn't stay because she had a baby to go to, and Ladeeta is afraid now of grandmother's house because he is a neighbor almost across the street and he said he'd kill her if she told and even though the police came and picked him up she thinks he will be back, he got big drug money to pay that jail bail, and his wife say, watch your back you asked for it, and so Ladeeta can't read and she wants a better life and her grandmother says she must go to school to have a better life and since February Ladeeta goes to school and stays at her sister's house and she doesn't go out and hang and she minds the baby washes the clothes and stays inside, keeps the house neat and clean, neat and clean, neat and clean

EXERCISE 42:

Dream House

Write the dreams of all the people who are sleeping in a house. It might be a house where you lived as a child, or it might be the house of a character about whom you are currently writing.

Gene Zeiger, who leads workshops based on this model, responded to this exercise by writing the following poem. In the final stanza, she includes the dream of the house itself.

Family

Their daily house is filled with fuss
over what is solid, with no room left
for the colored world which sits, lips
pursed, beyond the far away mountain.
At night, however, all lips part
and in the growing darkness

Mother dreams of figurines,
white China, and damask. An Arabian
merchant dusts her mahogany and, smiling,
kisses the red nails of her left hand.

Father dreams of wealthy stallions,
sleek and brass-belled. On a flat
vast plain without moon or cloud,
they pound and pound the shifting earth.

Little sister dreams of blue balloons
and the biggest one is hers. She picks
it up and flies to Paris. There she sits
in a sunlit room where everyone is breathing.

Older sister dreams of jungles

221

where she is wild, slim, and tragic.
Trees gleam with water and she can fly.
When the prince finds her, she never needs to smile.

The house dreams of animals:
cats stalking wildebeests, birds
preening on chairs. Cups and saucers
shatter to the floor as peacocks
stalk the sodden rubble, move slowly
out to the stunning trees.

EXERCISE 43:

A Poem as Trigger

Read one complete poem aloud, and then write. I have used many poems to trigger writing in my workshops. Sharon Olds' poem "The Takers," about a young girl who sits on her sister and pees on her, has evoked wonderful writing about sibling relationships. Raymond Carver's poem "Drinking while Driving" is a great stimulus to other writers.

Kathryn Dunn, who leads an Amherst Writers & Artists workshop at a high school for mainstream and refugee students, wrote in response to Sylvia Plath's poem "Daddy":

What would you say to your father
if he came back—if he could—
that you haven't already said
over and over, a thousand times
in his absence, like a rosary,
Hail Mary, Mother of God; keeping yourself
bound to him with your mantra, keeping
the feel of his hand on your shoulder,

carrying it always, not even knowing it.
What could you say to the man

you have held at the distance of one stiff arm
from the moment he died, with words like
he brought it on himself, and *son of a bitch.*
The man about whom you could only find hatred,
stunned by memories his death allowed.

What could you say to yourself
about allowing this man his faults,
his pain, when for fifteen years
that meant wronging yourself:
if he was bad, then you were alive;

if he was good, you were dead.
That was the formula—Hail Mary

Mother of God. What do you say
when you understand
the legacy that lives in your body
is yours, and the man who gave it to you
has died. Your hatred can no longer serve

his condemnation, or yours.
You must begin to find a way
into the legacy. Carry it, study it,
learn every corner and curve—
to do any less
will freeze the shoulder that feels his touch,
the arm that pushes him out.

You must begin with

what can you say to your father
you haven't already said.

Sense of Smell

Write in response to a strong odor. The sense of smell is said to be the most acute awakener of memories. When I am leading this exercise for a group of writers, I sometimes use the same odor (a mothball or a dab of Vicks Vaporub, for example). Little plastic containers for camera film are excellent to put samples in because you can ask the workshop participants to lift the lid and smell without looking at the source of the odor, therefore relying entirely on their sense of smell.

At other times, I have a variety of odors in small bottles: spices, motor oil, perfume, sachet, liquor, and so forth. There is a certain Thai fish oil that has been preserved underground for years before it is brought to the table. It has a powerful smell that to Western noses suggests decaying animal matter. Excellent for evoking strong memories!

Kate Nugent responded to the odor of a long stick of cinnamon:

> The clove-stuck orange hangs in Mom's closet like a barbed wire planet. It barely disguises the rum smell that emanates from the light brown stain on the beige carpet. Spiced rum was Grandma's favorite, I think as I pull out shoe boxes and sewing baskets from overhead, listening for the car in the driveway.
>
> I am looking for the proof, the bottle. The smell is spreading—it creeps beneath the plastic mushroom air freshener and the breath mints. It is the lowest smell there is. It's crawling under the foundation of the house and rising, intoxicating termites and mice with its fumes. I pick up a plastic Patriots' glass by the bedside that smells of vodka.

Where is that bottle? Not in the underwear drawer, toilet tank, or empty plastic vase. I want to see the hard copy behind the slurred voice on the telephone, the cigarette burns in the car upholstery. Ah, a locked metal box under the bed. I can't reach it— I can see that it's holding up the mattress.

What's the use? I don't need to see the Wild Turkey or the Beefeater—I don't need to approve of her brand. I want to know that she drinks. I want the evidence. But I already know that she's not just so tired that she fell asleep on the toilet and woke everyone with her snoring. Or that she's developed a speech impediment or that she is suddenly clumsy.

I need to find the bottle so I can confront her with it. I'll leave it on the kitchen table so it's the first thing she sees when she gets home. When she denies that she has a problem, I'll tell memories of Grandpa tipped over in his lawn chair, looking perplexed at the sky, ice cubes adorning his polo shirt like large crystal beads. Of Uncle Bob and his first wife and child who won't talk to him, even though he's in AA. Of Uncle Roy and his noon risings and Visine bottle in his breast pocket.

I want that bottle. I want to throw it from my bedroom window like I threw the picture of my father when he left so many years ago. I want her to cut her feet on the broken glass when she wanders around in the backyard with her slippers, whimpering and spitting and sucking on the ice from her drink.

EXERCISE 45:

Family Life

Write an intimate scene of family life. Begin with a simple description, and allow the writing to open up without forcing any "meaning" on it. The revelation of the habits of the grandmother at the end of this piece by Shelby

Gallier gives us an enormous amount of information about the time period of the story as well as about the world in which the child is growing up.

> The little girl will stay with Grandmother while Mother's in the hospital. When she is very very good, sometimes Grandmother lets her pick pansies and float them in the big shallow blue bowl on the front hall table. It is a special bowl, a Newcomb bowl. Grandmother's old teacher at the art school, Professor Woodward, made it. Grandmother says, "Look at the pansies' faces, darling. Cunning little purple and yellow faces smiling up at you." She holds the child up to see, and the child sees among the pansies her own small face reflected, blue eyes in the blue water of the blue bowl, all shining with afternoon.
>
> Before bed, they will go in Grandmother's little black-and-white tiled bathroom with the big gold faucets, and she will stand on the low stool with her tiny grandmother encircling her body, softly soaping each hand with Ivory. Grandmother's hands are always a little bit dirty too, because Grandmother is always digging in the yard.
>
> After they wash their hands, they will go into Grandmother's room and Grandmother will put her own nightgown over her head on top of all her clothes, then turn out the light and open the closet door and go into the closet. Inside the closet, with the closet door closed and the room all dark, Grandmother will take her clothes off under her nightgown. This is the best way to undress, so you can be sure you don't look down and see any naked parts of you. Grandmother always does it this way. Little girls don't have to, not until they get a little bit older.

EXERCISE 46:

The List

Make a list, and then write in response to your list. I suggest to my workshop one specific idea for a list, and mention that it can be from memory or imagined in relation to a character: everything in a medicine cabinet; items in a woman's purse or a man's pocket; things found under couch cushions; major fears; people who have made you angry; kinds of animals; names you would not choose for yourself; and so forth.

Carol Edelstein wrote this poem in response to an exercise given by Linda Spencer. Both women lead workshops based on the model described in this book. Linda's exercise was "make a list of the itemized expenses of an historical figure."

Very First Itemized Expenses

One rib (hers).
Fifty-five kilos grass and leaves, mixed varieties.
Seven years burbling brook.
Two walking sticks (hickory).
Rice, wheat, potatoes, maize —as needed.
Three conversations with God.
The tailfeathers of a gray parrot.
Eighteen fire-pits, seven with ocean view.
Eleven watertight gourds.
Twenty-five thousand hours of birdsong.
Carrots, celery, onions.
Kiwi fruit, raspberries, grapes—as needed.
Forty bulbs garlic.
Three hundred peppercorns.
One apple.
Two fig leaves.
One gate.
One backward glance (hers).

Sometimes a feeling of frustration in response to an exercise can be an effective trigger for writing, if the writer is willing to write down the feelings and images that come into his or her mind. Carolyn Pelletier used listing in a different way when she wrote the poem below in my Wednesday workshop in Amherst, expressing a feeling of being overwhelmed by "thousands of them everyday."

I am trying to save the pieces of the puzzle.
There are thousands of them every day.
Stories, objects, pictures, places, people,
They all fit into one giant whole.
Feelings, colors, words, dreams, visions,
That tell us what this is all about
What to expect, how to react,
Scoop up the past, project into the future,
Be in the now and celebrate.

The work is too much for me.
The pieces slip through my fingers,
The missing parts leave holes I cannot fill.
I have to give up putting it all together
And concentrate on the few pieces I have,
And celebrate imperfection.

FIVE-MINUTE EXERCISES

Sometimes a workshop comes to an end 10 or 15 minutes before the scheduled quitting time. When this happens, I give the option of writing again or leaving early. A few people always leave, and some always want to write. To those who stay, I offer a short writing time and we read to one another with very brief responses or no response.

If the workshop has been serious and you need a short writing exercise to close without changing the mood, have people write "free writing," without stopping, for a given number of minutes. Even when you mean something to be serious, though, funny things can happen. Once, when I used this exercise, I said, "Don't lift your pen from the paper for five minutes." The first woman to read had great trouble reading—she literally had not lifted her pen, and so all the words were connected to each other!

Another use for these short exercises is when a workshop needs to "loosen up" a bit or needs to laugh. The following exercises are for fun and for the natural humorists in your workshop who need to have their funny bones tickled now and then.

EXERCISE 47:

Pass the Dictionary

Pass around a dictionary. Each person closes his or her eyes and puts a finger down on a word. Each word is read aloud, and each person writes it down. In a short, timed writing, everyone is to write using as many of those words as possible.

EXERCISE 48:

Imaginary Definitions

Give everyone the same three or four obscure words, and five minutes to define them. Just read the definitions and enjoy the laughter, giving the real definition at the end. The dictionary is full of words which most of us would be hard-pressed to define.

The Imaginary Source

Everyone writes an imaginary source for one commonly used phrase, the source of which is obscure. A couple of books of origins of words and phrases kept on your library shelf can be a great resource. For example, the phrase *rule of thumb* evoked many interesting and funny imaginary origins in my workshop, not one of which was accurate. Cynthia Kennison whose fiction and plays have won national prizes, suggested this definition:

> It was King Wilfrum the Gauche who ordained that the length of his own left thumb would be the standard unit of measure for all things. It was a difficult standard to maintain because he often had difficulty telling his left from his right, and in winter both his thumbs shrunk slightly, and he could not be everywhere at once in his kingdom. "Rule of Thumb" has come to mean a rough, probably inaccurate guideline.

In fact, the phrase originated in British law: A man could legally beat his wife, as long as the stick with which he beat her was no bigger than his thumb!

The Accidental Name

Give everyone a three-by-five card. Have each person write a first name on the card and then pass it to the person on the right, who writes a last name. Collect the cards and pass them out at random, not letting anyone keep a card he or she wrote on. Tell them, "Now, you know everything about this person. You know what he or she dreamed last night, had for supper, fears, loves, hates. You know this character's favorite food, worst habit, and every secret. Just begin with one detail, and let it flow." Have people write about that character.

The following example is the first three paragraphs of a complete (very funny) short story written in a workshop by Paul Barrows about the name that he received on a card.

In September of 1975, Mr. Palermo and 198 other passengers disappeared while flying over the Bermuda Triangle. Subsequently, Mrs. Palermo discovered she could communicate with her husband by tuning her television to channel 28, a station unused in her local area. It was for this reason that Mrs. Palermo resisted getting cable TV, although she could tell by the tone of the salesman's voice when she explained this to him that he didn't believe a word of it. Well, what did she care?

It was Elaine's reaction that bothered her more. She had thought Elaine, her 16-year-old daughter, would be overjoyed when she said, "Sweetie, I've just talked to your father, he comes in now on channel 28." But instead, Elaine had just looked at her in horror. Well, Mrs. Palermo had finally decided, what else could one expect from a teenager?

This had all happened almost 20 years ago now, and after so much time, Mrs. Palermo was quite used to the whole thing. Of course, she had been afraid to get a new television—what if he would only come in on this one? He did not always come in clearly. Sometimes there was static, sometimes his voice was very faint. She often had to repeat her questions and occasionally she had to shout. But then, it had been like that even before he disappeared...

COMING FULL CIRCLE

I have a vision. There is a room in which 12 people sit, writing. One is a man in his 90s; one is a child of 10. Others are young adults, older adults. Every head is bowed over a page of paper. Half the hands in the room are spilling words out onto a page. After a while the writers read this new work to one another, and no one is made to feel embarrassed or ashamed. Then all of them bring out copies of a manuscript they were given the week before by one among them. Carefully, thoughtfully, kindly, the truth is spoken about where the strengths and problems lie. The author feels elated; she has been helped to see what to do next. She can hardly wait to go home and write again.

This vision is an actual experience that is happening in more and more classrooms, living rooms, and meeting rooms, because we are beginning to guess that we ourselves have something important to say. We are beginning to understand that we need to listen to voices across age, gender, race, social class, and educational levels. We are growing tired of hierarchies, tired of all the absentee landlords of our souls.

Writing belongs to the people—to you, to me. It is an extension of speech; it is an art form that every person has a right to use, perfect, and enjoy. A diversity of voices is a good thing for literature. The language of the woman in the U.S. Senate, the woman in the housing-project kitchen, the man in the spaceship, the farmer in the barbershop, the little girl singing as she swings in the schoolyard, the teenage boy calling to a friend as he rides his bicycle—these are the voices great literature is made of: the voices of our lives, as we live them and as we imagine them.

Anna Kirwan Vogel, poet, children's book author, and founding member of Amherst Writers & Artists, expresses it this way:

> If people can be brought into an attitude of trust, if they believe that their own words are sufficient for expressing truth as they experience it, then all the other work of writing will develop as naturally as the leaves bud on a morning-glory.
>
> When I say that in our workshops newly written material receives only positive discussion (we wait until it reaches manuscript form before offering any suggestions for change), a pitiful number of people assume that means no "real" work gets done. The discipline of this approach, though, opens the mind to the uniqueness of each human consciousness, the native language in which each conveys passion, curiosity, frustration, humor. Each person begins to see that there is never a set of words without its own specific gravity. Being asked to respond to what is there in the words, rather than what might still be lacking, reminds us that truth is always available, our omnipresent raw material. We can speak it. We can write it.
>
> Having faith in the power of our language is the same thing as having faith in people. With no more complicated ideas than truth and imagination, we hear each other's attempt to describe life, and we wish to match each other's courage. It is a lovely thing to hear a fierce or gentle story told when it's been just now committed to public words, words that have face.

In closing this book I want to tell a story from my Thursday-night workshop. I am forever looking for new objects with which to surprise my workshop participants. One day as I was walking in the woods near my home, I found some large burrs with the sharpest spines on them I had ever felt. The spines, or prickers, were wickedly sharp, but each burr had a "tail" or a floppy stem, about two inches long. Later I was told they were chestnuts; true chestnuts coming back all over this land after their destruction by blight. I handed them out and people wrote wonderful things in response. My ideas are usually pretty good. But not always.

One day in an antique shop I came upon 14 wooden rings tied together with an old piece of rope. Each ring had a little metal hook screwed into it. I brought them home, removed the hooks, dusted the rings, and was delighted with the grain of wood that shone in each. I thought I had found a treasure for the workshop. I hid them in a paper bag and handed them out one by one to the expectant writers. There was absolute silence. Everyone knew not to comment on the exercise because it might distract someone else from some association or memory. But this one was too much for Diane Garey, film-maker, poet, and my good friend. She is very funny, and when she cried out, "Pat, *I don't believe this.* You *aren't* giving us shower curtain rings!" everyone burst out laughing.

In truth I think Diane was right—it was not a very good writing exercise. But every exercise works for someone, and this one, with Diane's provocation, worked for me. I looked at the ring in my hand, and I saw how everything is so much more than what first appears to the casual eye. What I wrote is what I try to live; making of my writing workshops a place where we take the ordinary, everyday things, and in our ordinary, everyday speech make something new, something brave, something true. Or, as in the work below, just something that the writer wants to say.

Coming Full Circle

After giving twelve writers twelve antique wooden curtain rings as a writing exercise, and being greeted with blank expressions.

I give you wooden rings, wedding rings, rings of ancient trees cut down. I give you Ronald Reagan, saying of a giant Redwood, "If you've seen one tree, you've seen them all." I give you bathtub rings, earrings, fairy toadstool rings. I give you the whole friggin' fairy kingdom, Titania cuddling with an ass, Bottom braying in thousands of *Midsummer Night Dreams.* I give you dreams.

I give you Ring Around the Rosy, rings golden and tinkly above the heads of merry-go-round horses. I give you the ring of sweet mold around the circle of paraffin on your mother's wild blackberry jelly. I give you ringworm. I give you the ring of chapel bells in a monastery in Spain. I give you the entire Spanish inquisition; I give you a ring of blood around a sword hole in a young man's silken shirt.

I give you the round, open O of fishes' mouths, their bubbles, their green-blue beautiful eyes. I give you "Ring around the collar," Oprah, opera. I give you Saturday afternoon.

I give you the round hole a worm makes entering an apple. I give you the apple: stem, blossom, bright peel, sweet flesh, core. I give you the drain in your kitchen sink, the holes that hold the laces on the buckle-tongues of your grandfather's shoes. I give you cow pies in a field in Northern Ireland, the round O at the barrel mouth of an IRA man's gun. I give you a circle drawn around a date on a calendar in South Africa. I give you the steel washer around a small screw in a nuclear power plant at Three Mile Island.

I give you the pupil in the center of your own eye, everything you have ever seen, everything hidden behind your eyes. I give you the shape of the world. I give you the round, dark privacy of a squirrel's nest, knots in pine wood, rims of teacups, edges of dinner plates, clock faces, the letter O, the number 8, the shape of lips about to kiss.

I give you a wooden ring.

Take what the world gives you. Form it into words. Your writing is your art; it deserves the rest of your life in which to grow. You are a writer. A writer is someone who writes. Genius is in all of us, waiting to well up and overflow. Bríd Leonard, a young woman in my workshop in Sligo, Ireland, put into seven words the entire message of this book: "Write me a waterfall. Stand in it."

Index

About the Author

Pat Schneider is founder/Director of Amherst Writers & Artists and AWA Press. Her workshops are the subject of an award-winning documentary by Florentine Films, *Tell Me Something I Can't Forget*. Ms. Schneider has published two books of poetry, her plays have been produced more than 300 times in the United States and Europe, and her libretti have been recorded and performed by the Louisville Symphony and the Atlanta Symphony.